FULL OF BEANS

BY BROOKE DOJNY

FULL OF BEANS

HarperPerennial
A Division of HarperCollins*Publishers*

For Richard,
who is fortunately
a true
bean
aficionado

FIRST EDITION

Designed by Stephanie Tevonian

Library of Congress Cataloging-in-Publication-Data

Dojny, Brooke.
    Full of beans / by Brooke Dojny. — 1st ed.
        p.   cm.
    Includes index.
    ISBN: 0–06–095095–1
    1. Cookery (Beans) 2. Beans.   I. Title.
TX803.B4D68 1996
641.6'565—dc20   *95-37126*

96 97 98 99 00 ❖ / RRD 10 9 8 7 6 5 4 3 2 1

CONTENTS

ACKNOWLEDGMENTS

Thank you, especially, to Russ Parsons. His well-researched series of 1994 articles on beans in the Los Angeles Times was enormously helpful to me.

Many thanks to the California Dry Bean Advisory Board, the American Dry Bean Board, Native Seeds/SEARCH, and The Pillsbury Company.

And as ever, my deep appreciation to Bob Cornfield and Susan Friedland.

INTRODUCTION

Who would ever think, looking at a handful of dried beans—pebble-hard, utterly inedible—that when cooked, they are transformed into one of the most delicious foods on earth? That almost alchemic transmutation is but the first step on the fascinating road to discovering the sometimes hidden charms of legumes.

Beans are at long last finding the respect they deserve. High in protein, soluble fiber, vitamins, and minerals; low in fat; an excellent replacement for meat; the versatile medium for all manner of seasonings; *and* inexpensive, beans are being heavily touted by nutritionists and are suddenly the pampered darlings of restaurant chefs.

Home cooks are learning, too, about the many virtues of the legume, and are looking for sophisticated new, heart-healthy recipes, including revisions of classics as well as fresh approaches to the bean theme.

This book provides just that. American favorites such as Low Country Hoppin' John, Burgundy Street Red Beans 'n' Rice, and New England "From Scratch" Baked Beans are updated for the modern cook. Such international classics as Cassoulet with Herbed Pepper Crumb Crust, Havana "Moors and Christians," Soupe au Pistou, Pinto Bean and Jalapeño Quesadillas, and Gingered and Curried Red Lentils are translated and simplified for the American kitchen.

Beans are also used in new and fresh ways. Cannellini "Pesto" with Baguette Toasts, Angel's Hell-Fire Texas Black Bean Caviar, Black Bean and Sweet Potato Stew, Broiled Sea Bass on Green Lentil Salad, and Red Pepper Hummus are some of the contemporary recipes in the book.

BEAN TYPING

On a recent visit to my local specialty food market, I found all the common varieties of dried beans such as black, kidney, lentils, pinto, and navy beans. I also found Appaloosas, calypso beans, Swedish brown beans, Tongues of Fire, European soldier beans, rice beans, Maine yelloweyes, and wren's egg beans. Dozens and dozens of varieties exist, and, in an exciting new trend, growers such as Phipp's Ranch in California and Gary Nabhan at Native Seeds/SEARCH in Arizona are experimenting with cultivating heirloom beans that might have otherwise been lost to posterity.

Varieties in the color and shape of beans are their most noticeable characteristics, but subtle differences in flavor are also apparent. Here's a brief description of some of the most common beans.

BLACK BEANS. Small, kidney-shaped, and shiny black, these beans have an earthy flavor that some describe as mushroomlike. A staple ingredient in Latin American countries, black beans are becoming very popular here, as well. Also known as turtle beans.

BLACK-EYED PEAS. A cream-colored kidney-shaped bean with a purple black "keel," this bean is associated with southern U.S. cooking as well as Africa and India. Black-eyed peas are widely available frozen and are also dried.

CHICK-PEAS. Pale tan, firm, and nutty-tasting, these are popular in the Mediterranean, Middle East, and India. Chick-peas are the main ingredient in hummus, a famous purée or spread made with tahini. Chick-peas are also known as garbanzos and ceci.

CRANBERRY BEANS. Large, pale pink beans with beige mottling, cranberry beans turn an even pinky brown when cooked. They have a mild, sweet, nutlike flavor and are used extensively in Italian cooking. Cranberry beans can be used interchangeably with pinto beans. They are also known as Roman beans and borlotti beans.

DAL. Dal is the generic name in India for *all legumes*, including lentils, peas, and beans.

FAVA BEANS. A large, pale green, earthy-flavored bean, the fava is available fresh in the spring and is a rare seasonal treat when shelled and eaten fresh. The beans are removed from their large green pods, blanched in boiling water, and then the tough skins are removed. When dried, favas turn light brown. Favas are sometimes also known as broad beans, though technically they are similar but not identical.

GREAT NORTHERN BEANS. Small, oval white beans with a mild flavor and slightly mealy texture, these beans can almost always be interchanged in recipes with other white beans such as navy beans. They stand up well to long, slow cooking, and are often used for traditional baked beans.

KIDNEY BEANS. Large, sturdy, richly flavored beans that come in dark red, light red, and white. The red kidney bean is often used in the American Southwest in chili, the pink kidney bean is the "red bean" in New Orleans red beans and rice, and the white are the much-used Italian "cannellini."

LENTILS. Available in various colors, including green, brown, and red, lentils are one of the oldest known cultivated foods. The disk-shaped, quick-cooking lentil is used in countless dishes throughout the world.

MUNG BEANS. Native to Asia, these small round beans are used there primarily to make bean sprouts. In India they are dried and eaten either whole or husked and split (mung dal), where they are also known as black gram, split golden gram, and urad dal.

PINTO BEANS. Beige in color, with brownish streaks on the skin (resembling the coloration of a pinto pony), the pinto bean is associated with Mexican and South American cooking.

SPLIT PEAS. These are peas (both green and yellow) that are husked, dried, and split in half. Split peas need no soaking, and cook to a soft purée in soups in under an hour.

LEGUME LORE AND HISTORY

While I generally refer in this book to "beans," what I'm technically referring to are members of the legume family. Legumes — seeds that grow in a pod — include lentils, peas, split peas, and peanuts, as well as all of the beans such as soy, garbanzo, pinto, and many others.

Legumes are among the oldest foods known to mankind and can be traced as far back as the Bronze Age. In biblical lore, a dish of lentils and rice that is still a favorite in the Middle East is said to be the infamous "mess of pottage" for which Esau sold his birthright.

Before the extensive cross-pollination of foodstuffs that took place worldwide during the Age of Discovery, each portion of the globe cultivated its own types of beans — soy and mung in Asia, chickpeas, lentils, and fava beans in the Mediterranean, and all types of haricots (kidney beans, pintos, navy beans) in the Americas.

For millennia, beans have helped provide the cornerstone of the staple diets of large numbers of the world's people, with nearly every regional cuisine featuring delicious, nutritious bean dishes.

THE NUTRITIOUS BEAN

Beans have been called the "near-perfect food," and they play a key role in the USDA's Food Guide Pyramid. Beans are high in complex carbohydrates, nonmeat protein, and dietary fiber, and are chock-full of vitamins and minerals. All legumes are well endowed with B vitamins, including thiamine, niacin, riboflavin, B6, and folic acid, and some contain Vitamin A. In general, beans are rich in iron, calcium, phosphorous, zinc, and potassium.

Beans contain zero cholesterol and derive only 2 to 5 percent of their calories from fat (the exception being soybeans, which are about 34 percent fat). Additionally, some studies have actually shown that legumes can help control blood cholesterol by fighting the deposit of platelets in veins and arteries. Of course, the trace amounts of fat in beans, as in all vegetables, is of the polyunsaturated variety.

Eating meals rich in beans can help people on weight reduction diets. Beans are digested slowly, thus promoting a longer-lasting feeling of fullness by delaying the return of hunger pangs.

Because they provoke a lower insulin response than do other carbohydrates such as bread, cereals, potatoes, and pasta, beans can also be a real boon to diabetics and hypoglycemics.

While beans are our best nonmeat source of protein, the protein is incomplete, lacking the essential amino acid methionine (as is the case with all plant sources of food). Nutritionists don't worry too much about this missing amino acid, assuming that what you might miss in one meal, you make up in another.

STORAGE AND COOKING OF DRIED BEANS

Dried beans need to be rehydrated by cooking in simmering water. As with all ingredients from nature, many variables will affect the cooked result, including the age of the beans and how they've been handled and stored, the altitude at which the beans are cooked (at higher elevations they take longer to soften), and the degree of water hardness (more minerals can make for longer cooking times). Furthermore, acid ingredients such as tomatoes, vinegar, or citrus juices will greatly retard beans' cooking times if added early on during the cooking process.

Buy dried beans from a store with a high turnover to help ensure freshness, and store them in their original packaging or in a canister on a cool pantry shelf. Because I love beans' rainbow of colors and infinite variety of shapes, I display them in decorative glass jars on open shelving, but am aware that prolonged exposure to strong sunlight can dehydrate them further. I'm sure many of you have had the frustrating experience, as I have, of cooking beans that simply will not simmer to an edible softness no matter how long they cook. This probably means that the beans are old and/or were improperly stored and have become extremely dehydrated.

TO SOAK OR NOT TO SOAK?

For twenty-five years, I followed the conventional advice about the necessity of presoaking beans before cooking, and either soaked them overnight or, at the very least, employed the "quick soak" method of boiling for 2 minutes and then soaking for an hour before proceeding with the final cooking. The only cookbook author I'd ever read who didn't recommend presoaking was Mexican cooking expert Diana Kennedy, but I'd not previously tried her method.

Just before beginning work on this book, I heard about some research that Russ Parsons of the *Los Angeles Times* had done to test the conventional presoaking admonitions. Russ sent me the published results of his investigation, which concluded, in effect, that presoaking is completely unnecessary. I then proceeded to put *his* findings to my own tests. Net result? Russ's revolutionary discovery is indeed absolutely accurate. Presoaking beans shortens cooking times only marginally (about 30 minutes for most large beans) and although presoaked beans rehydrate slightly more evenly, there is very little noticeable difference in texture or taste.

Another myth debunked was discovering that adding salt to the cooking water does not appreciably lengthen the cooking time. (Russ also shoots down the theory that presoaking and rinsing cuts down on beans' gas-producing effects, but more about that later.)

I conducted dozens of tests using a variety of different types of dried beans. My recommendation is not to bother to presoak dried beans unless it's an old habit that is too ingrained to relinquish, or unless you really are thinking way ahead and want to shorten the final cooking time by a bit. (The "quick soak" method doesn't shorten the overall cooking time by the hour that it takes, so I don't bother with that at all.)

Before cooking any dried beans, rinse them in a strainer and pick out any dirt, tiny stones, or other debris. Since cooking times do seem shorter when you add the beans to already-boiling water rather than starting them in cold water, first bring the cooking water to a rapid boil, then add the beans and salt (or other salty ingredients such as ham bones). Bring to a second boil, reduce the heat to very low, and cook covered (extremely important) until tender. The range of cooking times I give in each recipe should take into account some variability in the dried beans, but if your beans are old, if the water is hard, or if you're cooking at a high altitude, times may be longer.

OF PRESSURE COOKERS, CROCKPOTS, AND MICROWAVES

Dried beans can be very nicely cooked in a pressure cooker. First, pick over and rinse the beans and presoak or not, as is your preference. Unless your pressure cooker is very large, cook only ½ pound of beans at one time. Add the beans, 4 cups of water, 1 tablespoon vegetable oil or olive oil (depending on whether you want the olive oil flavor in the final result), and ½ teaspoon salt.

(Adding the oil helps keep the beans from frothing too much.) Cook on high pressure (15 pounds) for approximately 7 minutes for lentils and split peas, 15 minutes for black beans and shell beans, and 25 to 35 minutes for larger beans such as kidney beans or pinto beans.

Either let the pressure cooker cool, off the heat, until the pressure is reduced, or run the pan under cool water to reduce the pressure rapidly. As with all cooking in the pressure cooker, the one inherent problem is not being able to see the food and gauge its degree of doneness until the pot is opened, but with a bit of practice, you'll learn how to estimate cooking times.

Beans can also be cooked beautifully in slow-simmering crockpots. Simply follow the manufacturer's directions. But do not try to cook dried beans in a microwave! The two are completely incompatible, and I really do not recommend it. However, already-cooked beans can be reheated extremely successfully in a microwave oven.

CANNED BEANS VS. COOKED FROM SCRATCH

Simmering good-quality dried beans "from scratch" to a melting tenderness is probably the ideal cooking method — and, in fact, in dishes where the dried beans will absorb flavors from other ingredients as in certain soups and stews, it's really a necessity. Tending a pot of Texas pot beans or constructing an elaborate dish such as Brazilian feijoada can be a soul-satisfying labor of love when you have the luxury of time (for many of us these days that's usually on weekends), but canned beans provide a quick and easy alternative when time is short.

I also happen to like them. For one reason, I think beans should always be cooked until tender. I deplore the tendency of some New American chefs to serve beans that are cooked al dente. Their texture is unpleasantly chalky, their flavor isn't fully developed, and they are utterly and disagreeably indigestible. Most canned legumes (as opposed to other canned vegetables) suffer not a bit in the texture or color department, and are only marginally less flavorful than their home-cooked counterparts. It does help to buy a better-quality canned product as opposed to store brands, and then drain and rinse them well in a strainer to remove residual "slime" and excess salt. Any nutrients that might be lost with rinsing are, I think, more than made up for in improved taste.

Canned beans are particularly well-suited — are, in fact, recommended — for making purées and dips. Their very soft texture means that they purée easily and smoothly, and also allows for better absorption of whatever seasonings are being used.

In this book, when I call for a quantity of "cooked beans" in a recipe, I always mean that you are free to use either cooked "from scratch" beans or drained canned beans. In certain recipes I'll suggest a "canned bean option" when it's appropriate.

BEANS, BEANS, THE MUSICAL FRUIT?

Okay, we need to come right out and say it: Beans can cause flatulence. One culprit is a complex sugar in legumes called an oligosaccharide, which is not digested in the stomach, and which breaks down into those unfortunate gases when it reaches the large intestine. The dietary fiber in beans (one of the reasons that they contribute to a healthy diet) also can result in similar gas-producing effects.

Conventional wisdom has suggested that presoaking beans and then cooking them in a change of fresh water "rinses" them of some of the offending complex sugars. Russ Parsons, in his impressively researched article for the *Los Angeles Times*, poked holes in this theory, and my (albeit informal) tests confirmed his finding that presoaking did nothing to reduce the gas-producing effects of beans. Furthermore, according to a researcher who has been studying beans for ten years at a USDA lab, the only effective method for extracting oligosaccharides involves boiling the beans for three minutes, rinsing them, and allowing them to stand, with three more rinses and changes of water, for a total of six hours before being cooked! In addition to being ridiculously impractical (not to mention extracting most of the good bean flavor), this method doesn't address the additional problem of the gas-producing dietary fiber in the legumes.

Net recommendations? Cook beans thoroughly, since tender beans are more digestible—and eat more beans! It is universally agreed that in cultures that routinely eat a diet rich in beans, people develop a tolerance for the offending sugars and fiber, sometimes affectionately known as "Mexican stomach."

BEAN CONVERSION TIPS

1 pound dry beans = 2 to 2½ cups

1 cup dry beans = 2 to 3 cups cooked beans

1 (19-ounce) can cooked, drained beans = 2 cups

1 (16-ounce) can cooked, drained beans = 1¾ cups

1 (15-ounce) can cooked, drained beans = 1½ cups

DELECTABLE APPETIZERS AND SNACKS!

All recipes in this chapter are vegetarian.

CANNELLINI "PESTO" WITH BAGUETTE TOASTS

About 1½ cups, 8 to 10 hors d'oeuvre servings

When I tasted a white *bean purée with basil similar to this at a recent "foodie" convention, I realized that the fresh basil added not only a boost of sunny Mediterranean flavor but also much-needed color to the white bean dip. For a big party I like to include this as part of a colorful trio of bean dips, along with Red Pepper Hummus and Zesty Black Bean Dip or Spicy Pink Adobe Dip, and I present them in hollowed-out peppers, cabbages, or eggplants.*

2 cups drained cooked white beans, such as cannellini or Great Northern, rinsed
1 cup packed basil leaves, plus additional for garnish
2 cloves garlic, peeled
3 tablespoons olive oil, preferably extra-virgin
1 teaspoon salt
¼ teaspoon black pepper
1 baguette, thinly sliced, or 1 package melba toast
Selection of fresh, cut-up vegetables such as fennel sticks, radishes, yellow pepper strips, and cucumbers

1) In the work bowl of a food processor, combine the beans, cup of basil, and garlic. Pulse to make a coarse purée. With the machine running, pour the olive oil through the feed tube and process to a smooth purée. Season with salt and pepper. Refrigerate for at least 2 hours to blend flavors. (Can be made 1 day ahead and refrigerated.) Bring to room temperature before serving.

2) Preheat the oven to 350 degrees. Arrange the bread slices (if using) in a single layer on a baking sheet and bake for 4 to 5 minutes until golden. Turn the bread and return to the oven for 4 to 5 minutes to toast lightly on the second side. Cool before serving. (Can be made 8 hours ahead and stored at room temperature in plastic bags.)

3) To serve, transfer the purée to an attractive serving bowl or hollowed-out vegetable such as an eggplant or cabbage. Garnish with sprigs of basil and serve surrounded by baguette toasts or melba toasts and raw vegetables, if desired.

RED PEPPER HUMMUS

2¼ cups, 15 to 20 hors d'oeuvre servings

Sesame seed paste, or tahini, lends richness and its distinctive, nutty flavor to this classic Middle Eastern chick-pea spread. Tahini can be purchased in health food stores or in the gourmet food section of many supermarkets. What is not classic about this version of hummus is the addition of roasted red peppers, which transform the color of the purée from creamy tan to an appealing pale, pinky orange hue. I use roasted red peppers from a jar here, and, because they're very soft, they purée beautifully.

2 cups drained cooked
   chick-peas, rinsed
½ cup drained roasted red
   peppers
⅓ cup tahini
2 cloves garlic, peeled
⅓ cup lemon juice
¾ teaspoon salt
¼ teaspoon freshly ground
   black pepper

¼ teaspoon ground cumin
8 small pita breads, white
   or whole wheat, cut in
   triangular eighths
Selection of fresh, cut-up
   vegetables such as cucumber
   slices, carrot and celery
   sticks, pepper strips

1) In the work bowl of a food processor, combine the chick-peas, red peppers, tahini, and garlic. Pulse to make a coarse purée. With the motor running, add the lemon juice through the feed tube, processing until the purée is smooth and slightly fluffy. Season with the salt, pepper, and cumin. Refrigerate for at least 2 hours to allow flavors to blend. (Can be made 3 days ahead and refrigerated.) Bring to room temperature before serving.

2) To serve, transfer the hummus to an attractive serving bowl or hollowed-out vegetable such as a large red pepper and serve surrounded with pita triangles and raw vegetables for dipping.

ZESTY BLACK BEAN DIP

About 1 cup, 6 to 8 hors d'oeuvre servings

In my area of Connecticut we're lucky to have several Hay Day stores, quality gourmet produce/food markets that were started by a local family a dozen years ago. Not only do the stores carry a wondrously extensive, and very fresh, assortment of dried beans, but they also make a couple of really delicious bean purées or spreads. This dip is my attempt at creating something similar to their spicy, darkly mysterious black bean spread. I don't remove the jalapeño ribs and seeds because I like this dip to be quite tongue-stingingly hot. If you prefer a gentler heat, scrape the ribs and seeds out.

1½ cups drained cooked black beans, rinsed
1 clove garlic, peeled
1 small jalapeño, fresh or pickled, cut in chunks
1 tablespoon red wine vinegar
1½ teaspoons Worcestershire sauce
1 teaspoon sugar
½ teaspoon chili powder
¼ teaspoon paprika
¼ teaspoon salt, or to taste
Packaged tortilla chips
Selection of fresh, cut-up vegetables such as jicama sticks, pepper strips, cucumber slices

1) In the work bowl of a food processor, combine the black beans, garlic, jalapeño, vinegar, Worcestershire, sugar, chili powder, and paprika. Process thoroughly to make a smooth purée. If the bean mixture is too thick to purée smoothly, add up to 1 tablespoon of water through the feed tube and process until smooth. (Some canned beans are drier than others.) Season with salt to taste. Refrigerate for at least 1 hour to allow flavors to blend. (Can be made 3 days ahead and refrigerated.) Bring to room temperature before serving.

2) To serve, transfer the bean dip to an attractive bowl or hollowed-out vegetable such as an acorn squash. Surround with tortilla chips and fresh vegetables for dipping.

BLACK BEAN CAKES WITH RAGIN' CAJUN SALSA

8 cakes, 4 appetizer servings

Jeremiah Tower made black bean cakes famous when he served them at his Santa Fe Bar and Grill in Berkeley, California. This version is a loose adaptation of his recipe from California the Beautiful Cookbook (Weldon Owen Inc., 1991). It's a truly inspired juxtapostion of flavors, textures, and colors — smooth, slightly sweet black bean cakes, topped with peppery-hot red and green salsa, and finished with a spoonful of tangy, cooling sour cream or crème fraîche. This makes one of the best first courses I've ever tasted!

BLACK BEAN CAKES

3 tablespoons olive oil
1 cup chopped onion
1 clove garlic, chopped
2¼ cups drained cooked black
   beans, rinsed
1 small jalapeño pepper, fresh
   or pickled, minced
½ teaspoon ground cumin
½ teaspoon salt
¼ teaspoon freshly ground
   black pepper
1 tablespoon honey
2 teaspoons red wine vinegar

Ragin' Cajun Salsa (recipe
   follows)
Approximately ½ cup sour
   cream or crème fraîche

1) Heat 1 tablespoon of the olive oil in a large nonstick or heavy cast iron skillet. Add the onion and cook over medium heat, stirring occasionally, until softened, about 5 minutes. Add the garlic and cook, stirring, for 1 minute. Add the beans along with the jalapeño, cumin, salt, pepper, and ½ cup water. Cook uncovered, stirring occasionally, until most of the liquid has evaporated, about 8 minutes. Add the honey and vinegar and continue to cook, stirring constantly, until the bean mixture is very dry and stiff, about 4 minutes.
2) Transfer the bean mixture to a food processor and process with short pulses to a coarse purée. Tranfer to a plate and press to make a large, flat cake. Place in the freezer until firm and cold, about

20 minutes, or refrigerate for at least 1 hour. (Bean mixture can be made 2 days ahead and refrigerated.)

3) Shape bean mixture into 8 cakes, each about 2½ inches in diameter. Heat the remaining 2 tablespoons of olive oil in a large, heavy skillet. Place the cakes in the pan in a single layer and cook over medium heat, turning once, until lightly browned on both sides and heated through, about 4 minutes. Do this in 2 batches if necessary.

4) To serve, place 2 cakes, slightly overlapping, on individual plates, spoon salsa over, and top each portion with a generous dollop of sour cream or crème fraîche.

RAGIN' CAJUN SALSA

About 2½ cups

1 large tomato, seeded and
    chopped (about 1½ cups)
Half a green pepper, seeded and
    chopped
½ cup thinly sliced scallions,
    including green tops
¼ cup chopped parsley
1 jalapeño pepper, fresh or
    pickled, minced

2 tablespoons peanut oil
½ teaspoon salt
½ teaspoon sugar
¼ teaspoon Tabasco
⅛ teaspoon cayenne pepper
⅛ teaspoon ground white pepper
⅛ teaspoon freshly ground
    black pepper

1) In a medium-sized bowl, combine the tomato, green pepper, scallions, parsley, and jalapeño pepper. Stir in the peanut oil and add the salt, sugar, Tabasco, and the cayenne, white pepper, and black pepper.

2) Let the salsa stand at cool room temperature for 30 minutes to blend flavors and release juices, or refrigerate. (Can be made up to 8 hours ahead and refrigerated.) Bring back to room temperature before serving over bean cakes.

SPICY PINK ADOBE BEAN DIP

*About 1¼ cups, 6 to 10 hors
d'oeuvre servings*

Pinto beans, widely used in Southwest cuisine, are a speckled brown and white in their dried state (like a pinto pony), but cook up to an even, pale, rust pink color, almost the shade of adobe. They make a lovely dip or spread, especially when enlivened with fiery hot "blackening" spice, a widely sold blend of several peppers and seasonings, and then smoothed and enriched with a bit of sour cream. Bright green chopped cilantro is stirred into this dip shortly before serving.

1½ cups drained cooked pinto
   beans, rinsed
Half a small onion, cut in
   chunks
1 clove garlic, peeled
1 teaspoon "blackening" spice
½ teaspoon sugar
¼ teaspoon ground cumin
¼ teaspoon salt
¼ teaspoon Tabasco

3 tablespoons regular or
   reduced-fat sour cream
3 tablespoons chopped cilantro
Packaged tortilla chips
Selection of fresh, cut-up
   vegetables such as celery
   sticks, bell pepper strips,
   and cauliflower florets

1) In the work bowl of a food processor, combine the beans, onion, garlic, blackening spice, sugar, cumin, salt, and Tabasco. Pulse to make a coarse purée. Add the sour cream and process until very smooth. Refrigerate for at least 1 hour to allow flavors to blend. (Can be made to this point 3 days ahead and refrigerated.) Stir in the cilantro and bring to room temperature before serving.

2) To serve, transfer the dip to an attractive bowl or hollowed-out vegetable such as a large red pepper. Surround with tortilla chips and fresh vegetables for dipping.

LYNN'S TRIPLE-LAYER TEX-MEX DIP

Approximately 10 hors d'oeuvre servings

*T*his hors d'oeuvre has a lot going for it: ease, simplicity, portability, great looks, and the spicy Tex-Mex flavors that appeal to almost everybody these days. At our family holiday parties, Lynn always brought this as her contribution to the snack table, and it was usually the first one to be devoured. You just use a chip to scoop right through all the layers, dredging up the whole array of flavors and textures in one bite! I think this dip is nice served cold in the summer, and warm in winter.

1 recipe Zesty Black Bean Dip (page 15) or 1 cup "Never-fried Beans" (page 64) or 1 cup canned refried beans
1 ripe avocado
2 tablespoons good-quality bottled salsa
1 cup sour cream
¾ teaspoon chili powder
¼ teaspoon ground cumin
1 cup seeded, diced fresh tomatoes
½ cup (2.25-ounce can) sliced or chopped black olives
⅓ cup thinly sliced scallions, including green tops
2 tablespoons chopped cilantro
1½ cups grated sharp Cheddar cheese
Tortilla chips

1) Spread the bean dip evenly in the bottom of a 9-inch glass pie plate or similar-size serving dish.

2) Peel and pit the avocado, cut into chunks, and mash on a plate with the salsa until well combined. Spread over the bean layer.

3) In a bowl, whisk the sour cream with the chili powder and cumin. Gently spread the cream mixture over the avocado layer.

4) Sprinkle evenly with the tomatoes, olives, scallions, and cilantro and top with the grated cheese. Chill for at least 1 hour to blend flavors. (Can be made up to 4 hours ahead and refrigerated.) Serve cold if desired.

5) To serve hot, bake in a preheated 400-degree oven until the cheese melts, about 15 minutes.

6) Place the pie plate on a large tray and surround with tortilla chips for dipping.

SWEET CORN, BLACK BEAN, AND RED PEPPER SALSA

***4 cups, about 8 hors d'oeuvre
or condiment servings***

Small, shiny black beans, crunchy chopped red pepper, and sweet golden corn kernels combine in this sublime salsa flavored with lots of garlic and chopped cilantro. It's a great example of the way young chefs are expanding on traditional Southwest cooking by using ingredients of the region in fresh, new dishes. I serve this both as an hors d'oeuvre with tortilla chips and as a condiment spooned liberally over grilled or roasted chicken, beef, or pork.

1½ cups drained cooked black beans, rinsed
1 cup thawed frozen corn kernels
1 large red bell pepper, seeded and chopped
¾ cup sliced scallions, including green tops
3 tablespoons olive oil

1 tablespoon lime juice
1 large clove garlic, minced
½ to 1 jalapeño pepper, fresh or pickled, minced
1 teaspoon sugar
½ teaspoon salt
¼ teaspoon freshly ground black pepper
½ cup chopped cilantro

1) In a large bowl, combine the beans, corn, red pepper, and scallions. Stir in the olive oil, lime juice, garlic, jalapeño, sugar, salt, and pepper and mix thoroughly. Refrigerate for at least 1 hour to blend flavors. (Salsa can be made 1 day ahead and refrigerated.)

2) Before serving, stir in the chopped cilantro.

STATE FAIR BLACK-EYED PEA AND SWEET ONION RELISH

3½ cups

This sweet-sour relish is absolutely delicious with hot dogs, grilled "brats," and hamburgers. If your market carries frozen black-eyed peas, I really recommend them. In my opinion, frozen black-eyed peas are superior to both cooked "from scratch" dried black-eyed peas and canned peas, because of their fresher taste.

1 (10-ounce) package frozen black-eyed peas, cooked according to package directions and drained (see Note)
1½ cups chopped Vidalia or other sweet onion
1 red bell pepper, seeded and chopped
½ cup chopped celery

½ teaspoon salt
¼ teaspoon dried red pepper flakes
½ cup cider vinegar
¼ cup packed light brown sugar
1 tablespoon dry mustard, preferably Colman's
¾ teaspoon mustard seed (optional)

1) In a large bowl, combine the black-eyed peas, onion, red pepper, celery, salt, and red pepper flakes.

2) In a medium-sized, nonreactive saucepan, combine the vinegar, brown sugar, mustard, and optional mustard seed. Bring just to a boil over medium-high heat, stirring to dissolve the sugar and dry mustard. Pour the hot liquid over the vegetable mixture and stir to mix well.

3) Let cool, transfer to a covered container and refrigerate for at least 1 more hour to allow flavors to blend. (Can be made 4 days ahead and kept refrigerated.)

4) To serve, use a slotted spoon to transfer relish to a bowl, leaving any excess liquid behind.

NOTE: If you can't find frozen black-eyed peas, use 2 cups drained cooked peas — either canned or cooked dried peas.

ANGEL'S HELL-FIRE TEXAS BLACK BEAN CAVIAR

3 cups

In Texas, of course, almost everything comes with a larger-than-life name or description, including the Lone Star version of "caviar." In fact, the small, shiny, black beans that are the basis of this relish do bear a faint resemblance to sturgeon eggs, so maybe the idea is not completely far-fetched. In true Texas style, this zesty condiment is almost lip-searingly hot, but you can adjust the amount of ground pepper if you like. It's fabulous as an accompaniment to any type of cooked meat and adds an interesting dimension to almost any sandwich.

2 cups drained cooked black beans, rinsed
1 cup chopped onion
1 red bell pepper, seeded and chopped
2 pickled jalapeños, chopped medium fine
1 clove garlic, finely chopped
⅓ cup red wine vinegar
1½ tablespoons sugar

1 teaspoon chili powder
¾ teaspoon dried savory
½ teaspoon ground cumin
½ teaspoon salt
¼ teaspoon freshly ground black pepper
¼ teaspoon cayenne
¼ teaspoon white pepper
1 tablespoon lemon juice

1) In a bowl, combine the beans, onion, red pepper, jalapeños, and garlic.

2) In a medium-sized nonreactive saucepan, combine the vinegar, sugar, chili powder, savory, cumin, salt, black pepper, cayenne, and white pepper. Bring to a boil over medium-high heat, stirring to dissolve the sugar. Add the black bean mixture, bring to a boil, stirring frequently, and simmer for 1 minute. Remove from the heat and stir in the lemon juice.

3) Transfer the mixture to a bowl and refrigerate until cold, about 1 hour. (Can be made 4 days ahead and kept refrigerated.)

4) Serve the relish cold or at room temperature.

PINTO BEAN AND JALAPEÑO QUESADILLAS

2 light main-course servings; serves 4 as an appetizer

Simple and tasty, these quesadillas make a great appetizer or light supper. If pinto beans are unavailable, almost any other kind of pink, red, or black bean can substitute. To serve as an hors d'oeuvre, cut each quesadilla into 6 or 8 wedges and pass with a salsa for dipping.

1½ cups drained cooked pinto beans, rinsed
¼ cup chopped onion
2 cups shredded hot pepper Monterey Jack cheese (8 ounces)
1½ teaspoons chili powder

¼ cup chopped cilantro, plus sprigs for garnish (optional)
4 (8-inch) flour tortillas
½ cup Pico de Gallo Salsa (page 80) or good-quality bottled salsa

1) Preheat the oven to 375 degrees.

2) In a bowl, combine the pinto beans, onion, and 2 tablespoons warm water. Use a potato masher or a fork to make a very coarse, spreadable mixture. In another bowl, toss the cheese with the chili powder and cilantro until well combined.

3) Place 2 tortillas on an ungreased baking sheet and spread with the bean mixture, spreading it to within about ½ inch of the edges. Sprinkle with the cheese mixture. Cover with the 2 remaining tortillas, pressing down firmly on the filling.

4) Bake in the preheated oven until the cheese melts and the tortillas are golden brown, 10 to 15 minutes.

5) Remove to a cutting board, cool slightly, and cut each quesadilla into 4 wedges (or 6 to 8 for appetizers). Top each wedge with a cilantro sprig, if desired, and pass a bowl of salsa at the table to serve with the quesadillas.

BLACK BEAN AND CHEDDAR NACHOS

3 to 4 snack servings; 2 light-meal servings

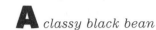

A *classy black bean variation of one of America's all-time favorite Tex-Mex foods, this nacho recipe lifts the genre well above the median standard. Serve with cold beer or a tart Margarita for a substantial appetizer that can turn into a light supper.*

BLACK BEAN PURÉE
1¾ cups drained cooked black beans, rinsed
¼ cup chopped onion
1 teaspoon chili powder
½ teaspoon ground cumin
¼ teaspoon Tabasco

NACHOS
3 cups shredded medium-sharp Cheddar cheese
¼ cup sliced pickled jalapeño peppers
½ cup chopped cilantro
1 (7- to 8-ounce) bag good-quality tortilla chips

1) To make the bean purée, combine the beans, onion, chili powder, cumin, and Tabasco in a food processor. Pulse to make a medium-smooth purée, adding 4 to 5 tablespoons water to make a mixture thin enough to be spooned or drizzled over the tortilla chips. (Can be made 2 days ahead. Cover and refrigerate. If necessary, warm in a microwave to thin to the correct consistency before using.)

2) Preheat the oven to 450 degrees.

3) For the nachos, toss the cheese with the jalapeños and cilantro. Spread the tortilla chips out on 2 approximately 9- by 12-inch heat-proof platters. (The chips will be a couple of layers deep.) Spoon or drizzle with the black bean mixture and sprinkle with the cheese mixture.

4) Bake in the preheated oven until the cheese melts and the chips are hot and tinged with darker golden brown, 7 to 10 minutes. Serve directly from the platters and eat out of hand.

SPLENDID BEAN SOUPS

*signifies vegetarian

BLACK BEAN SOUP WITH CHOPPED VEGETABLE GARNISHES

3 to 4 servings

Almost everyone seems to love this smooth, dark, black bean soup, particularly when it's presented with its colorful garnishes. If you serve it over a scoop of hot cooked white rice, it becomes an even heartier meal. Either cooked dried beans or canned black beans work just fine in this recipe.

BLACK BEAN SOUP

1 tablespoon olive oil

1½ cups chopped onion

1 large stalk celery, chopped

1 clove garlic, chopped

2 teaspoons dry mustard

3 cups drained cooked
   black beans

2 cups vegetable or chicken
   broth

3 tablespoons sherry

¼ teaspoon Tabasco

½ teaspoon salt

¼ teaspoon freshly ground
   pepper

GARNISHES

Chopped fresh tomato, chopped
   sweet onion, chopped
   cilantro, sour cream, or plain
   yogurt

1) In a large, heavy saucepan or soup pot, heat the olive oil. Add the onion, celery, garlic, and mustard. Cook over medium-low heat, stirring occasionally, until the vegetables are softened, about 5 minutes.

2) Add the beans and 3 cups of water. Bring to a boil, reduce heat, and simmer uncovered until the vegetables are very tender, 20 to 30 minutes.

3) In a food processor, process the soup until it is quite smooth. Return it to the cooking pot, add the broth, and simmer for 5 minutes, until heated through. The soup should be quite thick, but not so thick that it mounds on a spoon. Add liquid to thin if necessary. (Can be made 3 days ahead and refrigerated, or frozen. Reheat before serving, adding a bit of liquid to thin if necessary.)

4) Add the sherry and Tabasco and season with salt and pepper. Ladle into bowls and pass small dishes of the garnishes at the table.

SOUPE AU PISTOU

6 servings

This is the French version of minestrone, a thick, hearty brew, brimming with fresh garden vegetables and pasta. A spoonful of bright green pistou, the French cousin of pesto (but without the pine nuts) gets stirred into the soup just before serving. If you close your eyes, you can almost transport yourself to a sunny hillside in France overlooking the sea.

SOUP

8 ounces (about 1 cup) dried white beans such as cannellini, rinsed and picked over (see Note)

1 teaspoon salt, plus additional at end of cooking if necessary

1 (1-pound) can plum tomatoes with juice

2 carrots, thinly sliced

2 medium all-purpose potatoes, peeled and diced

1 leek, white and pale green part only, thinly sliced

2 cloves garlic, chopped

3 small zucchini, sliced

½ pound green beans, trimmed and cut in ¾-inch pieces

1 cup fresh or frozen green peas

2 ounces thin spaghetti, broken into 1-inch lengths

¼ teaspoon freshly ground black pepper

PISTOU

½ cup loosely packed basil leaves

2 cloves garlic, peeled

¼ cup grated Parmesan cheese

¼ cup olive oil

1) If you like, soak the beans in water to cover for 4 hours or overnight. Drain into a colander. In a large soup pot, bring 8 cups of water to a boil over high heat. Add the soaked or unsoaked beans and salt. Cover, reduce heat to very low, and simmer until the beans are almost tender, about 1½ to 2 hours.

2) Add the tomatoes, breaking them up into smaller pieces with the side of a spoon. Add the carrots, potatoes, leek, garlic, zucchini, and green beans. Bring back to a boil, reduce heat to medium-low, and cook uncovered until the beans and vegetables are tender, about 30 minutes. Add the peas at the end of the 30-minute cooking time. (Can be made 2 days ahead and refrigerated or frozen. Reheat before proceeding.)

3) If the soup is very thick, add 1 to 2 cups additional water before cooking the pasta. Add the spaghetti to the soup and simmer for about 10 minutes until the pasta is cooked al dente. Season with pepper and additional salt to taste. (Can be finished a couple of hours ahead. Reheat gently before serving.)

4) For the pistou, combine the basil, garlic, and cheese in the work bowl of a food processor. With the motor running, slowly pour the oil through the feed tube, stopping to scrape the sides once or twice, to make a smooth cream. Transfer to a small bowl. (Can be made a day ahead and refrigerated.)

5) To serve, ladle the soup into shallow bowls and top each serving with a spoonful of the pistou.

NOTE: Canned bean option: To make this soup with canned beans, omit Step 1 and add 3 cups drained cooked white beans to the salted water with the vegetables. Proceed with the rest of the recipe as written. I've made it using both, and can hardly tell the difference.

SPLIT PEA SOUP WITH HERBED YOGURT SWIRL

4 to 5 servings

If you can get fresh thyme, it adds a lively edge to this soul-satisfying soup, and the swirl of herbed yogurt at serving time is a welcome tart finish. In addition to being delicious, split peas are relatively quick-cooking dried beans, simmering to tenderness in a little over an hour.

SPLIT PEA SOUP
1 pound dried split peas, rinsed
2 smoked ham hocks or 1 meaty
    ham bone
4 cups chicken broth
1 bay leaf
1½ cups chopped onion
2 large or 3 small carrots,
    chopped
1 large rib celery, chopped
1 clove garlic, chopped

1½ tablespoons fresh thyme or
    1½ teaspoons dried
¼ cup chopped parsley
¼ teaspoon freshly ground
    black pepper
Salt
HERBED YOGURT
⅔ cup plain yogurt
1 tablespoon minced parsley
1½ teaspoons chopped fresh
    thyme or ½ teaspoon dried

1) Combine the split peas in a large soup pot with the ham hocks or bone, chicken broth, bay leaf, and 5 cups water. Bring to a boil over high heat, reduce heat to low, and cook covered until the split peas are almost tender, about 1 hour.

2) Add the onion, carrots, celery, garlic, thyme, and 2 tablespoons of the parsley. Cook uncovered over medium-low heat until the split peas and vegetables are tender, 30 to 40 minutes.

3) Remove the ham bones, strip the meat off the bones, and discard bones and fat. Chop the meat and return it to the soup. Discard the bay leaf.

4) Process the soup in a food processor in batches, pulsing to make a textured but not completely smooth purée. Add the remaining 2 tablespoons of parsley, and the pepper. Season with salt to taste. If the soup is too thick, add up to 1 cup or so of liquid to obtain the desired consistency. (Can be made 3 days ahead and refrigerated or frozen for up to 2 weeks. Reheat or thaw in a microwave or over low heat. Add a bit of additional liquid to thin if necessary.)

5) In a small bowl, whisk the yogurt with the parsley and thyme.

6) To serve, ladle the hot soup into bowls and top each with a spoonful of the yogurt. Use the tip of a small knife to swirl the yogurt slightly into the soup.

U.S. SENATE NAVY BEAN SOUP

5 to 6 servings

My research indicates that this savory white bean soup has been on the menu of the U.S. Senate restaurant since early in the century. My research also turned up about a dozen different variations of the recipe, from an absolutely bare-bones version calling for almost nothing but beans and water, to very complex concoctions. I've gone with one that uses all the best-sounding ingredients — and with excellent results. This soup makes a fantastic lunch on a chilly winter day, as many generations of senators will testify!

1 pound dried navy beans or other white beans such as Great Northern, rinsed and picked over (see Note)

1 meaty ham bone or 2 smoked ham hocks

1 bay leaf

1 teaspoon salt, or more to taste

2 cups chopped onions

1 medium all-purpose potato, peeled and chopped

2 carrots, chopped

2 stalks celery, chopped

2 cloves garlic, chopped

1 cup tomato sauce

1 teaspoon salt, or more to taste

¼ teaspoon freshly ground black pepper

1) If you like, soak the beans in water to cover for 4 hours or overnight. Drain into a colander. In a large soup pot, bring 10 cups of water to a boil. Add the soaked or unsoaked beans, ham bone, and bay leaf, bring to a boil, reduce heat to low, and cook covered until the beans are almost tender, 1½ to 2 hours. Remove as much meat as possible from the ham bone or ham hock, cut into small pieces, and return the meat to the pot. Discard the bone. Add the salt.

2) Add the onions, potato, carrots, celery, and garlic. Cook at a gentle simmer uncovered until the vegetables are very tender, 30 to 40 minutes. Add the tomato sauce and season with salt and pepper. Discard the bay leaf.

3) In a food processor, process about half the soup, pulsing to make a coarse-textured purée. Return the purée to the pot and adjust seasoning if necessary. (Can be made 3 days ahead and refrigerated, or frozen. Add a bit of additional liquid to thin if necessary.)

NOTE: Canned bean option: You can substitute 6 cups of cooked white beans, adding them in Step 2 along with 7 to 8 cups of water. I have found, though, that this soup really profited from long simmering with the ham bone, so I would recommend taking the extra time to cook from scratch here.

MOROCCAN HARIRA

6 servings

This hearty soup is traditionally served after sundown during the month of Ramadan to break each day's fast. Chock-full as it is with an abundance of meats, beans, grains, and vegetables, and enlivened with aromatic spices, harira clearly is as nourishing as it is tasty. This is one of those peasant soups with as many "authentic" versions as there are home cooks. With a thick slice of chewy peasant bread, harira makes a wonderfully satisfying and intriguingly exotic meal.

4 cups chicken broth
1 whole chicken breast, halved
½ cup brown or green lentils, rinsed and picked over
1 cinnamon stick
1 tablespoon olive oil
12 ounces lean lamb, cut in 1½-inch cubes
½ teaspoon salt
¼ teaspoon freshly ground black pepper
1½ cups chopped onions
3 cloves garlic, finely chopped

1½ teaspoons curry powder
¾ teaspoon powdered ginger
½ teaspoon crushed saffron threads
1 (28-ounce) can crushed plum tomatoes
2 cups drained cooked chick-peas
½ cup small pasta such as ditalini
2 tablespoons lemon juice
¼ cup chopped parsley
¼ cup chopped cilantro

1) In a large soup pot, combine the chicken broth, chicken breast, lentils, cinnamon stick, and 4 cups water. Bring to a boil, reduce the heat to low, and cook covered until the chicken is no longer pink in the center and the lentils are tender, about 25 minutes. Remove the chicken to a plate and, when cool enough to handle, shred the meat, discarding the skin and bones. Return the chicken to the pot with the broth and lentils.

2) In a large skillet, heat the olive oil over medium-high heat. Season the lamb with salt to taste and pepper and brown in the oil on all sides, about 5 minutes. Reduce the heat to medium, add the onions, and cook, stirring frequently, until softened and lightly browned, about 5 minutes. Add the garlic, curry powder, ginger, and saffron, and cook, stirring, for 1 minute, until fragrant. Scrape into the soup pot.

3) Add the tomatoes and chick-peas and cook partially covered over medium-low heat for 15 minutes to blend flavors. (The soup can be made ahead to this point. Refrigerate for up to 3 days, or freeze. Reheat before proceeding, adding a bit of additional water if necessary.)

4) Add the pasta and simmer until it is cooked, about 15 minutes.

5) Shortly before serving, stir in the lemon juice and the chopped parsley and cilantro. Taste and adjust seasonings if necessary.

CREAMY WHITE BEAN, CARROT, AND PEAR SOUP

4 to 5 first-course servings; 2 to 3 servings as a main course

Most *people won't guess that it's the addition of a bit of chopped pear that gives this lovely, smooth, golden-hued soup its slight sweetness and tantalizingly elusive flavor. It's a particularly versatile soup, delicious served either piping hot in cooler weather or chilled, as a first course, in the summer.*

1 tablespoon olive oil
1 cup chopped onion
2 cloves garlic, chopped
2 cups thinly sliced carrots
  (3 to 4 carrots)
1 tablespoon chopped fresh
  rosemary or 1½ teaspoons
  dried
4 cups vegetable or
  chicken broth

1 medium-sized firm pear (any
  type), peeled, cored, and
  chopped
2 cups drained cooked white
  beans such as cannellini or
  Great Northern, rinsed
½ teaspoon salt
¼ teaspoon freshly ground
  black pepper
¼ cup chopped parsley
1 cup milk, if serving cold

1) In a large, deep, heavy saucepan or soup pot, heat the olive oil over medium heat. Add the onion and sauté, stirring occasionally, until softened, about 4 minutes. Add the garlic and cook, stirring, until fragrant, about 1 minute. Add the carrots and rosemary, stirring to coat with oil. Add the broth, bring to a boil, reduce heat to low, and cook covered for 10 minutes.

2) Add the chopped pear and the beans and continue to cook until the carrots, pear, and beans are very soft, about 15 minutes.

3) Purée the soup in a food processor, in batches if necessary, pulsing until very smooth. Season with salt and pepper.
(Can be made 2 days ahead and refrigerated, or frozen.)

4) Reheat the soup over low heat if serving hot, adding a bit of additional liquid to thin if necessary. Ladle into bowls and sprinkle with parsley. If serving cold, thin the soup with the milk, ladle into bowls, and sprinkle with the parsley.

MRS. CORDISCO'S WHITE BEAN AND ESCAROLE SOUP

4 to 5 servings

This is the way my friend Mary Lu Cordisco's mother made this simple, soul-soothing Italian soup. When she had time, she cooked dried white beans from scratch, but drained canned beans work just fine here, too. I've tried omitting the extra step of blanching the escarole and adding it with the rest of the ingredients to cook in the soup, but find that it's just a bit too bitter for my taste. Finished with a sprinkling of freshly grated Parmesan cheese and accompanied by nothing more than a loaf of crusty bread, this is Italian comfort food at its best!

Salt

1 head escarole (1¼ to 1½ pounds), rinsed and torn or cut into bite-sized pieces (about 11 cups)

¼ cup olive oil

4 large cloves garlic, finely chopped

1¼ teaspoons dried oregano

¼ teaspoon dried red pepper flakes

7 cups chicken broth

4 cups drained cooked white beans such as cannellini or Great Northern

½ cup freshly grated Parmesan cheese

1) Bring a large pot of water to the boil, salt lightly, and add the escarole. Boil uncovered until tender, about 5 minutes. (This blanching removes some of the bitterness of the escarole.) Drain into a colander.

2) Meanwhile, in a large, heavy pot, heat the olive oil over medium heat. Add the garlic, oregano, and red pepper flakes and cook, stirring, until fragrant, about 1 minute.

3) Add the broth, white beans, and cooked escarole. Bring to a boil, reduce heat to medium-low, and simmer uncovered until the broth is slightly reduced and the flavors have blended. Taste and season the soup with salt to taste. None may be needed, depending on the saltiness of the chicken broth.

4) Serve in shallow bowls and pass the Parmesan cheese for sprinkling over the soup at the table.

PASTA E FAGIOLI

6 servings

When I started research-
ing pasta e fagioli (pronounced "pasta fazool" here), looking
for a recipe that would closely replicate the memorable
soup that I ate near Rome when I traveled there several years
ago, I found that Nancy Verde Barr's recipe came the closest.
Her wonderful book, We Called It Macaroni (Knopf, 1991),
contains not only marvelously workable recipes, but is full of
fascinating reminiscences of an Italian-American girlhood,
and replete with evocative photographs of a vanishing
time and place. You can provoke a heated debate by polling a
roomful of Italian-Americans about how they make "pasta
fazool" (more or less soupy, drained or undrained beans,
type of beans, which herb to use, and the like), so it's best
not to ask! But you certainly can't go wrong with this adaptation of Nancy's recipe.

2 tablespoons olive oil
2 ounces pancetta (unsmoked
  Italian bacon) or salt pork,
  minced (½ cup)
1½ cups finely chopped onion
1 stalk celery, finely chopped
3 large cloves garlic, finely
  chopped
1 tablespoon crumbled dried
  leaf sage or 2 teaspoons
  chopped fresh sage
¼ teaspoon dried red pepper
  flakes

5 cups chicken broth
1 (1-pound) can Italian-style
  chopped stewed tomatoes
  with juice
3 cups drained cooked white
  beans such as cannellini or
  Great Northern
¾ cup small dried pasta such as
  ditalini or tubetti
Salt
Freshly grated Parmesan cheese

1) In a large, heavy soup pot, heat the olive oil over medium-low
heat. Add the pancetta or salt pork and cook until the fat is rendered
but not browned, about 8 minutes. Add the onion and celery
and cook over medium heat, stirring occasionally, until the vegetables are soft, about 10 minutes. Add the garlic, sage, and red
pepper flakes and cook for 1 minute.

2) Add the broth, tomatoes, and beans. Bring to a boil over high heat, add the pasta, and reduce the heat to medium. Cook uncovered until the pasta is al dente, about 10 minutes. Taste and season with salt if necessary. (Leftovers can be kept for a couple of days in the refrigerator and reheated, but if making the soup ahead, don't cook the pasta until shortly before serving. It tends to absorb liquid and get soggy as it stands.)

3) Ladle into bowls and pass the Parmesan cheese at the table for sprinkling over the soup.

SIMPLIFIED GARBURE WITH FRESH THYME

4 to 5 servings

Garbure is one of those rustic, peasant soup/stews (in this case from the Pyrenees region of France), with as many recipes as there are farmers. To be a true garbure, it should be made with a special kind of slightly rancid(!) Basque salt pork and with confit of goose. Since neither is very likely to be available in our local supermarkets, I've devised this streamlined, Americanized, but still quite authentic-tasting version of one of the world's classic soups. It's nice presented with a lightly toasted and buttered slice of French bread on top.

4 slices bacon, coarsely
    chopped
1½ cups coarsely chopped onion
1 stalk celery, thinly sliced
4 cloves garlic, chopped
1 teaspoon dried marjoram
¼ teaspoon dried red pepper
    flakes
6 cups chicken or vegetable
    broth
5 cups thinly sliced cabbage
    (about ½ cabbage)
2 carrots, thinly sliced

2 cups diced yellow turnip
    (about ½ medium-sized
    rutabaga)
2 cups diced red-skin potato
    (1 medium-large potato)
2 cups drained cooked white
    beans such as cannellini or
    Great Northern
2 tablespoons chopped fresh
    thyme or 2 teaspoons dried
Salt
½ cup chopped parsley, prefer-
    ably flat-leaf Italian parsley

1) Cook the bacon over medium-low heat in a large, heavy soup pot until the fat is rendered and the bacon is crisp, about 8 minutes. Remove the bacon with a slotted spoon, leaving 2 tablespoons drippings in the pot. Reserve the bacon.

2) Add the onion and celery to the bacon drippings and cook, stirring occasionally, for 5 minutes, until somewhat softened. Add the garlic, marjoram, and red pepper flakes and cook, stirring, for 1 minute.

3) Add the broth, cabbage, carrots, turnip, potato, beans, and thyme. Bring to a boil over high heat, reduce heat to medium-low, and cook partially covered at a gentle simmer until all the vegetables are tender, 25 to 30 minutes. Taste and season with salt. (Can be made 2 days ahead and refrigerated. Reheat before serving, adding a bit of additional liquid to thin if necessary.)

4) Stir in the parsley. Ladle into bowls, sprinkle with the reserved bacon if desired, and serve.

HESTER'S LENTIL SOUP

8 to 10 servings

My *mother made this richly satisfying, down-to-earth lentil soup every winter as I was growing up, and I was known to polish off several bowls at one sitting! It makes a wonderful cold-weather supper, with some crusty bread and a big green salad on the side.*

1 pound (about 2½ cups) lentils, rinsed and picked over
1 meaty ham bone or 1 small smoked pork butt (about 1¼ pounds)
2 cups chopped onion
1 cup chopped celery
2 medium carrots, thinly sliced
2 large cloves garlic, finely chopped
2 (16-ounce) cans stewed tomatoes, crushed

2 bay leaves
1 tablespoon dried thyme
½ teaspoon freshly ground black pepper
Salt
½ cup chopped parsley, preferably flat-leaf Italian parsley
2 tablespoons cider vinegar
2 tablespoons olive oil (if ham bone is not used)

1) In a large soup kettle, combine the lentils, ham bone or pork butt, and 10 cups of water. Bring to a boil over high heat, reduce heat to low, and simmer covered until the ham and lentils are tender, about 1 hour. Remove the ham bone or pork, dice the meat, and discard the bone, if used. (You should have about 2 cups of meat.) Return the meat to the soup.

2) Add the onion, celery, carrots, garlic, tomatoes, bay leaves, and thyme. Cook uncovered at a gentle simmer over medium-low heat until the vegetables are tender, about 30 minutes. Season with pepper and salt to taste. The soup should be quite thick. If too thick, thin with broth or water. If too thin, continue cooking for a few more minutes to reduce. (Can be made 3 days ahead and refrigerated, or frozen. Reheat gently before serving, adding liquid if necessary.)

3) Before serving, remove the bay leaves and stir in the parsley and vinegar. If the soup was made with the boneless pork butt and not the ham bone, stir in the olive oil. (The ham bone adds a bit more fat to the soup.) Ladle into bowls and serve.

MANY-BEAN CHILI SOUP

6 servings

I find the prepackaged mixtures of many beans very appealing. Usually they comprise as many as ten or fifteen varieties, with different colors and shapes and sizes. I like the fact that some of the beans cook faster than others, thereby thickening the soup as they "melt," while the longer-cooking beans retain their shape and texture to the end. Here's a terific, full-flavored, quite spicy soup with traditional chili seasonings.

1 pound (about 2½ cups) packaged mixed dried beans, rinsed and picked over	2 tablespoons dark brown sugar
	2 teaspoons chili powder
	1 teaspoon ground cumin
8 ounces kielbasa or other garlicky smoked sausage	½ teaspoon dried oregano
	½ teaspoon powdered mustard
2 medium onions, chopped	2 tablespoons lemon juice
1 stalk celery, chopped	2 teaspoons cider vinegar
1 bay leaf	¼ teaspoon Tabasco, or to taste
1 (8-ounce) can tomato sauce	Salt, if needed

1) If you like, soak the beans in water to cover for 4 hours or overnight. Drain in a colander. In a large soup pot, bring 10 cups of water to a boil. Add the soaked or unsoaked beans, reduce the heat to low, and cook covered for 1 hour.

2) Add the kielbasa in one piece, along with the onions, celery, and bay leaf. Continue to simmer for 30 minutes.

3) Add the tomato sauce and stir in the brown sugar, chili powder, cumin, oregano, powdered mustard, and lemon juice. Continue to cook covered until the beans are tender, 30 to 60 minutes. Remove the kielbasa, split in half lengthwise, and cut into thin slices. Return to the soup. Adjust the thickness of the soup if necessary. If too thick, add more liquid; if too thin, cook uncovered to reduce slightly. (Can be made 3 days ahead and refrigerated. Freezing is not recommended because the kielbasa flavor becomes too strong. Reheat before serving, adding a bit of additional liquid to thin if necessary.)

4) Before serving, discard the bay leaf, stir in the vinegar and Tabasco, and taste for seasoning. Ladle into bowls and serve.

SWEET PEA, POTATO, AND LEEK SOUP

4 servings

This lovely, delicate, green pea soup makes a terrific meatless meal when made with vegetable broth. It's equally delicious served hot or cold, with some French bread and a cherry tomato and sweet onion salad.

2 tablespoons butter
2 large leeks, white and pale green parts only, washed and thinly sliced
2 medium-large (10 to 12 ounces each) russet or all-purpose potatoes, peeled and coarsely chopped

4 cups vegetable or chicken broth
2 cups frozen or fresh peas
1 teaspoon dried tarragon
1½ cups half-and-half or milk
Salt
¼ teaspoon white pepper
3 tablespoons snipped chives

1) Heat the butter in a large, heavy saucepan or soup pot. Add the leeks and cook over medium heat, stirring occasionally, until tender, about 7 minutes. Add the potatoes and broth and bring to a boil. Reduce the heat to low and cook covered for 15 minutes. Add the peas and tarragon and continue to simmer until the peas and potatoes are tender, 6 to 12 minutes. (Fresh peas, particularly if large, will take the longer cooking time.)

2) Purée the soup base in a food processor, in batches if necessary, pulsing to make a fairly smooth purée. (Can be made 2 days ahead to this point and refrigerated.)

3) If serving hot, heat the base in a saucepan over medium heat, add the milk, and heat through. If serving cold, stir milk into the base. Season with salt and white pepper.

4) Ladle the soup into bowls and top each serving with a sprinkling of snipped chives.

SPRIGHTLY BEAN SALADS

*signifies vegetarian

MOROCCAN TOMATO AND CHICK-PEA SALAD

4 to 6 servings

This salad dressing, fragrant with cumin and cayenne and other aromatic spices from North Africa, tranforms the humble chick-pea and some chopped vegetables into something wonderfully exotic. Fresh mint adds its clean, clear taste as a balance to the intensity of the spicing. It's a perfect summer lunch main course or side salad partnered with anything grilled — but is particularly delicious with grilled lamb.

MOROCCAN DRESSING

2 tablespoons lemon juice
1 tablespoon white wine vinegar
1 teaspoon ground cumin
1 teaspoon paprika
½ teaspoon cayenne
½ teaspoon salt
¼ teaspoon freshly ground
    black pepper
¼ cup olive oil

TOMATO AND CHICK-PEA SALAD

2 cups drained cooked chick-
    peas, rinsed
2 medium tomatoes or 1 large
    tomato, seeded and chopped
    (about 2 cups)
2 cups seeded, diced cucumber
    (preferably with some skin
    left on)
¾ cup chopped red onion
⅓ cup chopped fresh mint

1) To make the dressing, combine the lemon juice, vinegar, cumin, paprika, cayenne, salt, and pepper in a large mixing bowl. Whisk in the olive oil until blended.

2) Add the chick-peas, tomato, cucumber, and red onion to the dressing. Stir to mix well. Refrigerate for at least 1 hour. (Can be made 1 day ahead.)

3) Just before serving, fold chopped mint into the salad and taste for seasoning, correcting if necessary.

MINTED CHICK-PEA, COUSCOUS, AND OLIVE SALAD

4 to 6 servings

Couscous makes an excellent warm-weather salad component. Not only is it delicious, but it needs only a quick 5-minute soak to soften and "cook." In this recipe the couscous is tossed with nutty chick-peas, chopped fresh vegetables, black olives, and tangy feta cheese. The dressing uses lots of fresh mint, another favorite summertime herb. In Morocco, where couscous originated, a salad like this might be presented on romaine lettuce leaves, which can then also serve as "scoops" for eating the salad out of hand. I've served this as part of a summer buffet to rave reviews.

FRESH MINT DRESSING
¼ cup lemon juice
1 clove garlic, peeled
1 teaspoon Dijon mustard
¼ teaspoon salt
¼ teaspoon freshly ground pepper
¼ teaspoon sugar
¾ cup mint sprigs
⅔ cup olive oil

COUSCOUS AND CHICK-PEA SALAD
1 cup packaged couscous
½ teaspoon salt

2 cups drained cooked chick-peas, rinsed
1 large red bell pepper, seeded and thinly sliced
1 large carrot, finely diced
⅔ cup chopped red onion
½ cup pitted good-quality black olives, such as kalamata
1½ cups coarsely crumbled feta cheese (6 ounces)
Romaine lettuce leaves
Mint sprigs for garnish

1) In the work bowl of a food processor, combine the lemon juice, garlic, mustard, salt, pepper, sugar, and mint sprigs. Pulse to chop garlic and mint. With motor running, slowly pour the olive oil through the feed tube to make a smooth dressing.

2) In a medium saucepan, bring 1½ cups water to a boil. Add the couscous and salt, stir once, remove from the heat, and let stand, covered, for 5 minutes, until the water is absorbed and the couscous softens.

3) Transfer the couscous to a large bowl and fluff grains with a fork. Add the chick-peas, red pepper, carrot, onion, and olives. Pour the dressing over the salad and toss to combine. Add the feta and stir gently to mix. Refrigerate for at least 1 hour. (Can be made 3 hours ahead, but the mint will darken on longer standing.)

4) Taste the salad for seasoning and adjust if necessary. Line a platter with romaine leaves, spoon the salad over, and garnish with mint sprigs.

SISTER'S COVERED-DISH FOUR-BEAN SALAD

6 to 8 servings

This classic American picnic salad endures decade after decade for many good reasons. It's attractive, easy to prepare, can be made well ahead, is easily transported to a picnic, and (most important of all), the salad tastes great! Almost everyone has a favorite family recipe, and this is ours, updated and freshened up a bit, dressed with a tangy sweet-sour vinaigrette that is a good deal less sweet than many. The recipe is easily multiplied to feed a crowd.

CIDER VINAIGRETTE
¼ cup cider vinegar
2 tablespoons sugar
2 teaspoons grainy Dijon mustard
2 cloves garlic, minced
½ teaspoon salt
¼ teaspoon freshly ground black pepper
¼ teaspoon Tabasco
½ cup vegetable oil

FOUR-BEAN SALAD
8 ounces green beans, trimmed and cut in 1½-inch lengths
8 ounces yellow wax beans, trimmed and cut in 1½-inch lengths, or 1 (10-ounce) package frozen beans
1½ cups drained cooked chick-peas, rinsed
1½ cups drained cooked kidney beans, rinsed
1 red or green bell pepper, seeded and chopped
1 cup chopped red onion

1) To make the dressing, combine the vinegar, sugar, mustard, garlic, salt, pepper, and Tabasco in a large mixing bowl. Whisk until the sugar dissolves. Whisk in the vegetable oil.

2) Cook the green and wax beans together in a large pot of rapidly boiling salted water until tender, about 6 minutes. Drain into a colander.

3) Add the hot beans, chick-peas, kidney beans, bell pepper, and onion to the salad bowl and toss to mix well. Refrigerate for at least 2 hours. (Can be made a day ahead.)

4) Before serving, taste salad and adjust seasonings if necessary.

SAVORY ROMAN BEAN AND ZITI SALAD

4 servings

Roman beans, also known as cranberry beans, are kidney-shaped, mottled tan in color when dry, and an attractive brownish-pink when cooked. They're mild, sweet-tasting beans, which in Italy are often used in soups and in combination with pasta. This simple and satisfying pasta and bean salad is seasoned with savory (fresh, if you can obtain it, dried if you can't), called "the bean herb," because its flavor has a particular affinity for beans of all kinds. The salad makes a terrific summery supper.

SAVORY BALSAMIC VINAIGRETTE

2 tablespoons balsamic vinegar
1 teaspoon Dijon mustard
1 large clove garlic, minced
1½ tablespoons chopped fresh savory or 1 teaspoon crumbled dried
½ teaspoon salt
½ teaspoon freshly ground pepper
¼ cup olive oil, preferably extra-virgin

ROMAN BEAN AND ZITI SALAD

8 ounces dried ziti or other large pasta
3 cups drained cooked Roman, red, or kidney beans, rinsed
1 green bell pepper, seeded and coarsely chopped
½ cup chopped Italian parsley
Sprigs of fresh savory, if available, for garnish

1) To make the dressing, combine the vinegar, mustard, garlic, savory, salt, and pepper in a large mixing bowl. Whisk in the olive oil until blended.

2) Cook the pasta in a large pot of rapidly boiling salted water until al dente, about 10 minutes. (If you are using fresh savory, add a sprig to the cooking water.) Drain in a colander and rinse under cold water to cool.

3) Add the pasta, beans, and green pepper to the salad bowl and toss to combine. Add the parsley and toss again. Refrigerate for at least 1 hour. (Can be made 6 hours ahead and refrigerated.)

4) Before serving, taste for seasoning, correcting if necessary. Garnish with sprigs of savory, if available.

BLACK-EYED PEA SALAD WITH SUN-DRIED TOMATO VINAIGRETTE

6 servings

Black-eyed peas have a uniquely sweet, pealike flavor and buttery-smooth texture that combines well with the assertive, almost smoky flavor of sun-dried tomatoes. With a trio of chopped vegetables added for crunch and color, this salad combination turns up a real all-season winner. Pass a basket of warm cornbread or corn muffins for a simply super supper.

SUN-DRIED TOMATO VINAIGRETTE

¼ cup balsamic vinegar
2 teaspoons grainy Dijon mustard
1 clove garlic, minced
2 teaspoons honey
¼ teaspoon freshly ground pepper
¼ cup olive oil
½ cup slivered oil-packed sun-dried tomatoes, drained, with 1 tablespoon sun-dried tomato packing oil reserved

BLACK-EYED PEA SALAD

2 (10-ounce) packages frozen black-eyed peas
1 red bell pepper, seeded and chopped
1 cup thinly sliced celery
⅔ cup chopped red onion
½ cup chopped parsley
1 bunch arugula or tender dandelion greens

1) To make the dressing, combine the vinegar, mustard, garlic, honey, and pepper in a large mixing bowl. Whisk until honey dissolves. Whisk in the olive oil and stir in the sun-dried tomatoes and sun-dried tomato oil.

2) Bring lightly salted water to a boil in a large saucepan. Add the peas and cook over medium heat until just tender, 15 to 20 minutes. Drain into a colander and run under cold water to cool.

3) Add the black-eyed peas, red pepper, celery, onion, and half the parsley to the mixing bowl and stir to mix well. Refrigerate at least 30 minutes. (Can be made 6 hours ahead and refrigerated.)

4) Taste the salad and adjust seasonings if necessary. Line a shallow bowl with greens, heap salad in the center, and sprinkle with the remaining parsley.

RED BEAN AND BROWN RICE SALAD WITH HOT PEPPER DRESSING

6 to 8 servings

A *takeoff on the famous New Orleans Red Beans 'n' Rice, this healthful salad is made with red beans, nutty brown rice, and lots of fresh vegetables. The dressing recipe, as given, is* quite *peppery, but its kick can be adjusted up or down by varying the amount of ground pepper to suit your palate. Vegetarians can easily omit the smoked ham for a truly delectable meatless dish.*

HOT PEPPER DRESSING

3 tablespoons white wine
    vinegar
2 teaspoons grainy Dijon
    mustard
1 large clove garlic, minced
1½ tablespoons chopped fresh
    thyme or 1 teaspoon dried
½ teaspoon freshly ground
    black pepper
¼ teaspoon white pepper
¼ teaspoon cayenne
¼ teaspoon salt, or to taste
⅓ cup olive oil

RED BEAN AND BROWN RICE SALAD

3 cups cooked brown rice
    (see Note)
2 cups drained cooked red
    beans or kidney beans,
    rinsed
1 cup diced smoked ham
    (4 ounces)
2 medium tomatoes or 1 large
    tomato, seeded and diced
    (about 2 cups)
1 green bell pepper, seeded
    and chopped
¾ cup sliced scallions, including
    green tops

1) To make the dressing, combine the vinegar, mustard, garlic, thyme, black, white, and red peppers, and salt in a large mixing bowl. Whisk in the olive oil until blended.

2) Add the rice, beans, ham, tomato, green pepper, and ½ cup of the scallions to the dressing and toss gently to combine. Refrigerate at least 30 minutes. (Can be made 1 day ahead and refrigerated.)

3) Before serving, taste for seasoning and add more salt if necessary. (The amount of salt needed will depend on the saltiness of the ham and the amount of salt used in cooking the rice.) Sprinkle with the remaining ¼ cup of scallions before serving.

NOTE: Use regular or quick-cooking brown rice.

"ROMAN BEANS" CENTRO SALAD

4 servings

One of my favorite restaurants in Connecticut is Centro, a lovely Italian bistro, and probably my all-time favorite dish there is a mixed bean salad that they call "Roman Beans." The chef, David Rutigliano, was kind enough to share his recipe, which I've adapted here for home cooks. Although it's listed on the menu as an appetizer, it's plenty hearty enough for a main course, so I usually just team the bean salad with a soup or green salad, leaving room for a dessert of biscotti and Vin Santo!

1½ ounces diced pancetta or thick-sliced bacon (about ⅓ cup)

5 tablespoons plus 1 teaspoon olive oil, preferably extra-virgin

4 cloves garlic, peeled and smashed (see Note)

1½ cups drained cooked Roman or red beans, rinsed

1½ cups drained cooked black beans, rinsed

1½ cups drained cooked butter beans (large lima beans), rinsed

2 tablespoons lemon juice

¼ teaspoon freshly ground black pepper

Salt

1 large bunch arugula

3 tablespoons chopped Italian parsley, plus parsley sprigs for garnish

1 lemon, cut in 4 wedges

1) In a large skillet, cook the diced pancetta in 1 teaspoon of the olive oil over low heat until the bacon is crisp and the fat is rendered, about 10 minutes. Remove the bacon with a slotted spoon to a plate. Pour off the grease but do not wash the pan.

2) In the same pan, heat the remaining 5 tablespoons of olive oil and the smashed garlic over low heat until the garlic turns a pale golden brown, about 10 minutes. Watch carefully so the garlic doesn't scorch. Remove the garlic with tongs, leaving the garlic oil in the pan.

3) Add the Roman, black, and butter beans to the garlic oil, raise the heat to medium-high, and toss gently until heated through, 3 to 4 minutes. Add the pancetta and lemon juice and stir gently to combine. Season with the pepper and salt to taste. (The beans may not need salt as the pancetta can be quite salty.)

4) Make a bed of arugula on a serving platter or on individual plates. Spoon the warm beans over the greens and sprinkle with the parsley. Garnish each serving with a lemon wedge and a sprig of parsley. Squeeze additional lemon juice over the salad if desired.

NOTE: This salad is flavored subtly with garlic. For a more assertive garlic flavor, mince one or two of the cooked cloves of garlic and stir into the salad.

WARM LENTIL AND SAUSAGE SALAD

6 servings

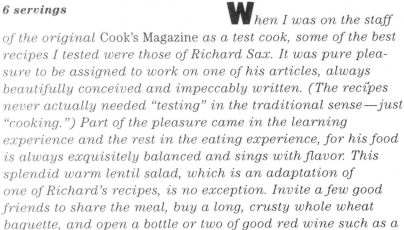

When I was on the staff of the original Cook's Magazine as a test cook, some of the best recipes I tested were those of Richard Sax. It was pure pleasure to be assigned to work on one of his articles, always beautifully conceived and impeccably written. (The recipes never actually needed "testing" in the traditional sense—just "cooking.") Part of the pleasure came in the learning experience and the rest in the eating experience, for his food is always exquisitely balanced and sings with flavor. This splendid warm lentil salad, which is an adaptation of one of Richard's recipes, is no exception. Invite a few good friends to share the meal, buy a long, crusty whole wheat baguette, and open a bottle or two of good red wine such as a Barolo—now there's a recipe for a happy evening!

2 cups lentils, preferably French green lentils, rinsed and picked over
2 cups chicken broth
1 carrot, cut in chunks
½ rib celery
1 pound garlicky smoked sausage such as kielbasa or andouille, cut in ½-inch slices
¼ cup balsamic vinegar
2 teaspoons lemon juice
½ cup olive oil
¼ teaspoon freshly ground pepper
1 (7-ounce) jar roasted red peppers, cut in strips
⅔ cup sliced scallions, including green tops
½ cup pitted black imported olives such as niçoise
1 bunch arugula, washed and trimmed
Salt

1) In a medium saucepan, combine the lentils, chicken broth, carrot, celery, and 2 cups water. Bring to a boil, reduce the heat to low, and cook, covered, until the lentils are tender but not mushy, 25 to 45 minutes. (French green lentils will take 10 to 15 minutes longer to cook than brown lentils.) Discard the carrot and celery and drain off any remaining liquid. (Can be cooked a day ahead and reheated.)

2) Meanwhile, cook the sausage in a large skillet over medium-low heat, stirring frequently, until well browned and cooked through, about 12 minutes. Remove with a slotted spoon to a plate, leaving any browned bits and about 1 tablespoon of fat in the pan. (Sausage can be cooked several hours ahead and reheated in a microwave before proceeding.)

3) Add the vinegar and lemon juice to the pan drippings and gradually whisk in the olive oil. Season with pepper. Pour all but about 2 tablespoons of the warm dressing over the warm lentils and set aside for about 5 minutes so the dressing is absorbed.

4) Transfer the lentils to a serving platter. Spoon the cooked sausage slices over the lentils, and scatter with the red peppers, scallions, and olives. Spoon the remaining dressing over the salad and arrange the arugula around the edge of the platter.

5) Serve immediately, passing the salt shaker at the table, though the salad will probably not need it as the sausage and olives can be quite salty.

BLACK BEAN, SHRIMP, AND MANGO SALAD

4 main-course servings;
6 to 8 buffet servings

S*piked with the vibrant flavors of the tropics, this salad also makes a dazzlingly beautiful presentation with its hot pink, shiny black, orange, and red hues. Serve it as an elegant summer main course, either on individual plates or from a shallow, leaf-lined serving platter as a stunning addition to a buffet.*

TROPICAL DRESSING
¼ cup lime juice
1 tablespoon white wine vinegar
1 teaspoon Dijon mustard
2 cloves garlic, minced
2 teaspoons chili powder
2 teaspoons ground cumin
½ teaspoon salt
½ teaspoon freshly ground
    pepper
⅓ cup olive oil

BLACK BEAN, SHRIMP, AND MANGO SALAD
4 cups drained cooked black
    beans, rinsed

1 red bell pepper, seeded and
    chopped
1 ripe but firm mango, peeled
    and cut in ½-inch dice
    (see Note)
½ cup chopped fresh cilantro
¾ cup thinly sliced scallions,
    including green tops
1 pound large or medium
    shrimp, shelled and deveined
    (see Note)
3 cups torn greens such as a
    mixture of romaine and
    arugula

1) To make the dressing, combine the lime juice, vinegar, mustard, garlic, chili powder, cumin, salt, and pepper in a large mixing bowl. Whisk in the olive oil until blended. Remove and set aside ¼ cup of dressing to use as the shrimp marinade.

2) Add the beans, red pepper, mango, cilantro, and ½ cup of the scallions to the salad bowl and stir gently to combine with the dressing. Refrigerate for 30 minutes to 1 hour until thoroughly chilled. (Can be made 6 hours ahead, but if so, add the mango, cilantro, and scallions not more than 1 hour before serving.)

3) Prepare a medium-hot charcoal fire or preheat a gas grill. Toss the shrimp with the reserved ¼ cup of tropical dressing and marinate for 15 to 30 minutes. Thread the shrimp onto skewers and grill, turning once or twice, until lightly charred outside and no longer translucent within, about 6 minutes.

4) Line a shallow bowl or platter with greens. Spoon bean salad over greens, top with the shrimp, which has been removed from the skewers, and sprinkle with the remaining ¼ cup of scallions.

NOTE: To prepare the mango, cut slices of the unpeeled fruit from around the large pit and then score the flesh into ½-inch squares while it is still attached to the peel. Turn inside out so that the skin is now concave, and use a sharp knife to cut the diced fruit from the skin.

As an alternative to grilling the shrimp, you can poach them in lightly salted water in a saucepan until cooked through, cool, and then marinate in the reserved ¼ cup of dressing.

TUSCAN TUNA AND CANNELLINI SALAD

3 to 4 servings

Leave it to those fabulous Tuscan cooks to come up with something so simple that tastes this good. The bland white beans counterposed with the salty tang of tuna, flavored with nothing more than a drizzle of simple, lemony vinaigrette, and, ergo, a meal that, while created by peasants, is fit for a king! If you like, serve the salad on a bed of arugula, which dresses it up a notch.

1 (6-ounce) can oil-packed tuna
3 cups drained cooked
    cannellini or other white
    beans, rinsed
¾ cup chopped red onion
1 tablespoon lemon juice
1 tablespoon white wine vinegar
2 teaspoons chopped fresh
    oregano or ½ teaspoon dried

¼ teaspoon freshly ground
    pepper
3 tablespoons olive oil,
    preferably extra-virgin
½ cup chopped Italian parsley
Salt, if necessary
3 ripe tomatoes, cut in wedges

1) Drain and discard all but about 1 tablespoon oil from the tuna. In a large mixing bowl, combine the beans and chopped onion. Add the tuna with its remaining oil and flake into large chunks with a fork.

2) In a small bowl, combine the lemon juice, vinegar, oregano, and pepper. Whisk in the olive oil until blended.

3) Pour the dressing over the salad and stir gently to combine, being careful not to break up the tuna too much. Refrigerate for at least 1 hour. (Can be made 1 day ahead.)

4) When ready to serve, stir in the parsley and taste and correct seasonings if necessary, adding salt to taste. Serve on plates or from a platter, surrounded by tomato wedges.

BURRITOS, TOSTADAS, PIZZAS, AND SANDWICHES

*CHILI BEAN SLOPPY JOES . 63

"NEVER-FRIED" BEAN BURRITOS WITH LIME-GRILLED CHICKEN . 64

*SPICED ORANGE, RAISIN, AND BLACK BEAN TOSTADAS . 66

BEEF AND BEAN TORTILLA PIZZAS WITH TOMATO-ORANGE SALSA . 68

*GRILLED PIZZAS WITH CANNELLINI, TOMATOES, AND OLIVES . 70

*FALAFEL IN PITA POCKETS WITH MIDDLE EASTERN SALAD . 72

*signifies vegetarian

CHILI BEAN SLOPPY JOES

6 sandwiches,
3 to 4 supper servings

Beans replace meat in this delightfully messy all-American favorite supper sandwich. You can start eating these with your hands, but soon you'll be licking your fingers or needing to resort to a knife and fork — and/or lots of napkins. Some purists prefer Sloppy Joes lettuceless, but I like the crisp, fresh iceberg crunch.

2 tablespoons vegetable oil
1 cup chopped onion
1 green bell pepper, seeded and
 coarsely chopped
2 cloves garlic, chopped
1½ teaspoons chili powder
1 teaspoon dried thyme
1 (14- to 16-ounce) can stewed
 tomatoes with juice
2 cups drained cooked kidney
 beans or other red or pink
 beans

1 tablespoon ketchup
1 tablespoon cider vinegar
1 teaspoon Worcestershire
 sauce
6 hard rolls or kaiser rolls, split
 and lightly toasted
2 cups shredded iceberg lettuce
 (optional)

1) In a large skillet, heat the vegetable oil and cook the onion and green pepper over medium heat until softened, about 5 minutes. Add the garlic, chili powder, and thyme and cook, stirring, for 1 minute. Add the tomatoes, beans, and ½ cup of water. Bring to a boil, breaking up the tomatoes into smaller chunks with the side of a spoon. Reduce the heat to low and cook covered for 15 minutes to develop the flavors.

2) Use the back of a spoon to mash about a quarter of the beans against the side of the pan to thicken the mixture. Stir in the ketchup, vinegar, and Worcestershire and simmer uncovered over medium heat until the mixture is thick enough to be spoonable, adding a little more water if the sauce is in danger of sticking to the pan. (Can be made 3 days ahead and refrigerated. Reheat before serving.)

3) Spoon some sauce over the bottom half of each roll, sprinkle with the optional lettuce, and cover with the top halves of the rolls.

"NEVER-FRIED" BEAN BURRITOS WITH LIME-GRILLED CHICKEN

8 burritos; 4 supper servings

I *developed these "never-fried" beans as an alternative to refried beans, that high-fat Tex-Mex staple ingredient. "Never-fried" beans are easier to make, too, and I think they taste every bit as good as the traditional version (and infinitely better than canned refried beans). Here they're used in conjunction with lime-grilled chicken in these scrumptious burritos. Put all the toppings out in separate dishes and let people compose their own.*

"NEVER-FRIED" BEANS
2 cups drained cooked pinto
    beans, rinsed
½ cup chopped red onion
1 pickled jalapeño, chopped
1 teaspoon chili powder
½ teaspoon ground cumin
Salt and pepper

BURRITOS
1½ tablespoons lime juice
1 tablespoon vegetable oil
½ teaspoon grated lime zest

¼ teaspoon salt
⅛ teaspoon freshly ground
    pepper
2 skinless, boneless chicken
    breast halves (about
    6 ounces each)
8 (7- to 8-inch) flour tortillas
1 cup Pico de Gallo Salsa
    (page 80) or good-quality
    bottled salsa
2 cups shredded romaine or
    iceberg lettuce

1) To make the beans, combine the pinto beans, onion, jalapeño, chili powder, and cumin in a food processor. Pulse to make a coarse purée, adding 2 to 3 tablespoons warm water to thin to a spreadable consistency. Season with salt and pepper if necessary. The beans can also be mashed to a coarse purée in a bowl, using a large fork or potato masher. (Set aside at room temperature, or refrigerate for up to 3 days. Bring back to room temperature before using.)

2) In a shallow dish, stir together the lime juice, vegetable oil, lime zest, salt, and pepper. Add the chicken breasts, turning to coat, and set aside to marinate for 20 to 60 minutes. (Do not marinate for more than about an hour, or the lime juice will begin to break down the meat.) Wrap up all the tortillas in a piece of foil.

3) Prepare a medium-hot fire in a charcoal grill or preheat a gas grill. Set the tortillas at the edge of the grill to heat. Grill the chicken, turning once or twice, until golden brown outside and white but still moist inside, 8 to 10 minutes total. Remove to a cutting board, cool for a few minutes, and cut into thin crosswise slices.

4) To make the burritos, spread about ¼ cup of room temperature "never-fried" beans on each warm tortilla. Add a few slices of chicken, spoon on some salsa and lettuce, and roll into a loose cylinder. Eat out of hand.

SPICED ORANGE, RAISIN, AND BLACK BEAN TOSTADAS

8 tostadas; 4 supper servings

Since raisins are the same color as black beans, they remain an elusive presence in this unusually delicious tostada topping, contributing just a hint of sweetness along with the fragrant spices and orange juice and zest. Spraying tortillas with vegetable oil and baking rather than frying them cuts down on fat as well as eliminating the most time-consuming and messy part of tostada-making.

SPICED ORANGE, RAISINS, AND BLACK BEANS

2 tablespoons olive oil
1½ cups chopped onion
2 cloves garlic, finely chopped
2 jalapeño peppers, fresh or pickled, minced
1 teaspoon ground cumin
½ teaspoon ground coriander seed
3 cups drained cooked black beans, rinsed
¾ cup raisins
2 teaspoons grated orange zest
¼ cup orange juice
½ teaspoon salt
¼ teaspoon freshly ground pepper

TOSTADAS

8 (6-inch) corn tortillas
Vegetable oil spray
2 cups shredded romaine or iceberg lettuce
2 cups grated medium-sharp Cheddar cheese
1 cup Pico de Gallo Salsa (page 80) or good-quality bottled salsa

1. For the beans, heat the olive oil in a large skillet. Add the onion and cook over medium heat until it begins to soften, about 4 minutes. Add the garlic, jalapeños, cumin, and coriander and cook, stirring, for 1 minute. Add the beans, raisins, and ¾ cup of water. Bring to a boil, reduce the heat to medium-low, and simmer uncovered, stirring occasionally, until somewhat thickened, about 8 minutes. Stir in the orange zest, orange juice, salt, and pepper. Use a wooden spoon to mash about half the beans against the side of the pan to thicken the mixture. Simmer about 5 minutes longer, until the mixture is thick and of a spreadable consistency, adding a bit more water if needed. (Can be made up to 2 days ahead. Cover and refrigerate. Reheat before using.)

2) Preheat the oven to 375 degrees.

3) Spray the tortillas lightly on both sides with the vegetable oil spray and arrange in a single layer on one or two baking sheets. Bake in the preheated oven until crisp and pale golden brown, 8 to 10 minutes.

4) Spread warm tortillas with black beans and top with lettuce, cheese, and salsa.

BEEF AND BEAN TORTILLA PIZZAS WITH TOMATO-ORANGE SALSA

8 pizzas; 4 supper servings

n interesting and deli-cious tomato-orange salsa turns these tortilla pizzas into a festive meal, one that is certainly special enough for guests. Add a rice side dish and additional condiments such as small bowls of sour cream, chopped avocado, and black olives for a truly celebratory meal. I've also served these pizzas — with or without the salsa — cut into small wedges as a very tasty hors d'oeuvre.

TOMATO-ORANGE SALSA

1 large seedless orange
1 large plum tomato
½ cup chopped red onion
¼ cup chopped fresh cilantro
¼ teaspoon black pepper,
    preferably coarsely ground
¼ to ½ teaspoon Tabasco

BEEF AND BEAN PIZZAS

½ pound ground round or chuck
1 cup chopped onion
1 tablespoon chili powder
1 teaspoon ground cumin
1 teaspoon dried oregano
2 cups drained cooked pinto,
    kidney, or red beans
8 (7- to 8-inch) flour tortillas
2 cups shredded hot pepper
    Monterey Jack cheese
    (8 ounces)

1) To make the salsa, grate 1 teaspoon of zest from the orange into a small bowl. Peel the orange, coarsely chop it, and transfer to the bowl with the orange zest and as much of the orange juice as you can scoop up. Core and chop the tomato and add to the bowl along with the onion, cilantro, pepper, and Tabasco, using the larger amount if you want more heat. Stir to combine. Set aside to allow flavors to blend for at least 15 minutes. (Can be made several hours ahead and refrigerated. Bring back to room temperature before serving.)

2) To make the filling, in a large skillet, cook the ground beef and the onion over medium to medium-high heat, stirring frequently, until the meat loses its pink color. Add the chili powder, cumin, and oregano and cook, stirring, for 1 minute. Add the beans, along with ¾ cup of water. Bring to a boil, cover, reduce heat to low, and cook for 10 minutes. Uncover the pan and cook over medium heat for 5 minutes, mashing about half of the beans against the side of the pan with a spoon to thicken the mixture. The topping should be quite thick but not sticking to the pan. Add a small amount of additional water if necessary. (Can be made 2 days ahead and refrigerated. Bring back to room temperature before using.)

3) Preheat the oven to 425 degrees.

4) Place the tortillas in a single layer on two large baking sheets and bake for 2 to 3 minutes, until lightly toasted.

5) Divide the bean topping among the tortillas, spreading it almost to the edges, and sprinkle with the cheese.

6) Return the pizzas to the oven and bake until the edges are crisp and the cheese melts, 4 to 6 minutes. Cut each pizza into halves or quarters and pass the salsa at the table.

GRILLED PIZZAS WITH CANNELLINI, TOMATOES, AND OLIVES

2 supper servings;
3 to 4 snack servings

Anyone who has ever been fortunate enough to eat the wood-grilled pizzas at George Germon and Johanne Killeen's restaurant Al Forno in Providence, Rhode Island, remembers the experience. Although by now I'm sure other chefs are doing it, they were the first to successfully perfect the technique of cooking pizzas directly over a fire rather than in traditional ovens. Their toppings, too, represent combinations of some of the best of the simple, pure Italian ingredients that we've come to appreciate so much. This recipe, which uses refrigerated pizza dough, is obviously a simplified adaptation, but it was inspired by ideas in George and Johanne's excellent book, Cucina Simpatica *(HarperCollins, 1991).*

1 cup drained cooked white beans such as cannellini, rinsed
3 tablespoons olive oil, preferably extra-virgin
2 cloves garlic, minced
½ teaspoon dried rosemary, crumbled
1½ cups chopped, seeded tomatoes (1 large tomato)

¼ cup pitted imported black olives, such as niçoise
3 tablespoons chopped Italian parsley
3 tablespoons grated Romano or Parmesan cheese
1 (10-ounce) package refrigerated pizza dough

1) Prepare a medium-hot fire in a charcoal grill or preheat a gas grill. Be sure the grids are well seasoned or oiled.

2) In a bowl, combine the beans, olive oil, garlic, and rosemary. Using a potato masher or fork, mash to a rough purée. In another bowl, toss the tomatoes with the olives. In a third bowl, toss the parsley with the cheese.

3) Unroll the pizza dough and use your hands or a rolling pin to stretch it to a rough 10- by 15-inch rectangle. Cut with a large knife into quarters. Place on a well-oiled platter or baking sheet.

4) Use a large spatula to transfer the dough, oiled side down, to the grill. Cook, lifting frequently with tongs to check for possible burning, until the undersides are crisp, with nice brown grid marks, 2 to 4 minutes. Turn the pizzas and move them to the cooler edges of the grill. Spread with the bean purée, scatter evenly with the tomato/olive mixture, and sprinkle with the parsley/cheese mixture. Move to the hotter center of the grill, cover the grill, and cook until the bottom crusts are crisp and brown and the topping is hot and tinged with brown. Serve hot.

NOTE: To cook in the oven, preheat the oven to 425 degrees. Press the dough (in one roughly rectangular piece) into an oiled 10- by 15-inch jelly roll pan. Top with beans, tomatoes, and cheese. Bake until the crust is golden brown on the bottom and the toppings are hot and tinged with brown, 12 to 15 minutes. Cut in wedges to serve.

FALAFEL IN PITA POCKETS WITH MIDDLE EASTERN SALAD

4 servings

Eaten all over the Middle East, and now in this country in cities with any sizable Middle Eastern population, falafel are savory, spiced chick-pea fritters. I like them best nestled in a pita pocket, topped with crunchy fresh vegetable relish and nutty tahini sauce. Tahini is available in the specialty food section of most supermarkets and a can or jar will keep almost indefinitely on the refrigerator shelf. The oil separates out on standing, so just be sure to stir it vigorously before you use it.

TAHINI SAUCE
½ cup tahini
1 clove garlic, peeled and
    smashed
¼ cup lemon juice

MIDDLE EASTERN RELISH
1 medium-large tomato, seeded
    and chopped (about 1 cup)
¾ cup peeled and seeded
    cucumber
½ cup chopped green bell
    pepper
2 teaspoons lemon juice
½ teaspoon chili powder
½ teaspoon sugar
¼ teaspoon salt
⅛ teaspoon freshly ground
    pepper

FALAFEL
4 cups drained cooked
    chick-peas
2 cups coarsely chopped onion
2 cloves garlic, peeled
½ cup fine dry bread crumbs
3 tablespoons all-purpose flour
2 teaspoons ground cumin
2 teaspoons ground coriander
    seed
1½ teaspoons dried oregano
½ teaspoon turmeric
½ teaspoon cayenne
½ teaspoon salt
¼ teaspoon freshly ground
    black pepper
Vegetable oil for shallow-frying
8 (6- to 7-inch) pita breads

1) To make the tahini sauce, combine the tahini, garlic, and lemon juice in a food processor, and pulse to chop the garlic into smaller pieces. Add ¼ cup cold water and process until a smooth, creamy sauce forms. Transfer to a serving bowl. (The sauce will keep, refrigerated, for several days.)

2) For the relish, stir together the chopped tomato, cucumber, green pepper, and lemon juice. Season with the chili powder, sugar, salt, and pepper. (Can be made 3 hours ahead and refrigerated.)

3) For the falafel, in a food processor combine the chick-peas with the onion, garlic, bread crumbs, flour, cumin, coriander, oregano, turmeric, cayenne, salt, and pepper. Process, scraping down the sides 2 or 3 times, until the mixture is very smooth and relatively lump-free. Scrape into a bowl and refrigerate for at least 15 minutes. (Can be made 1 day ahead.)

4) In a large, heavy skillet, preferably cast-iron, heat ½ inch of vegetable oil over medium heat to 350 degrees. (If a cube of bread browns in about 30 seconds, the oil is ready.) Shape the falafel mixture into 1½-inch balls and flatten slightly to make 2-inch patties. (You should have approximately 32 patties.)

5) Cook the patties in the oil, in two or three batches if necessary, until golden brown, 2 to 3 minutes per side. Remove with a slotted spoon and drain on paper towels. (Falafel can be transferred to a baking sheet and kept warm in a 275-degree oven for 20 minutes.)

6) Cut the pitas in half, fill each pocket with two falafel patties, and spoon in relish and tahini sauce.

SCRUMPTIOUS MAIN DISHES CHILIS STEWS, AND

PENNE WITH SAVORY BEAN AND BACON SAUCE

4 servings

Seasoned with dried savory and just a bit of smoky bacon, this sauce is great spooned over penne or any other stubby, chewy pasta. Add a green salad and perhaps some seeded breadsticks and you've got a terrific weeknight (or any night) supper.

4 slices bacon, coarsely
  chopped
1½ cups chopped onion
1 green bell pepper, seeded and
  coarsely chopped
2 cloves garlic, finely chopped
2 (14- to 16-ounce) cans stewed
  tomatoes
1½ to 2 cups drained cooked
  kidney beans, rinsed

1 cup dry white wine
2 teaspoons dried savory
½ teaspoon salt
¼ teaspoon freshly ground
  pepper
12 ounces dried penne
¼ cup grated Parmesan cheese

1) In a large skillet, fry the bacon over medium heat, stirring occasionally, until it is crisp, about 8 minutes. Remove with a slotted spoon, leaving the drippings in the pan. Add the onion, green pepper, and garlic and cook, stirring frequently, until softened, about 5 minutes.

2) Add the tomatoes with their juices, breaking them up with the side of a spoon if they are in large pieces. Add the beans, wine, savory, salt, and pepper. Cook the sauce uncovered over medium-low heat until it is somewhat thickened and the flavors blend, about 15 minutes.

3) Meanwhile, cook the pasta in a large pot of boiling salted water for about 10 minutes, or until al dente. Drain in a colander.

4) Stir the reserved bacon into the sauce and taste for seasoning, adding more salt and pepper if needed.

5) Spoon the sauce over the pasta and pass the cheese at the table.

ITALIAN SAUSAGE AND WHITE BEANS ON ARUGULA

4 servings

Some would label this a salad, others a main course, but all would call it delicious. It's a wonderful quick little meal that really is elegant enough, in a peasant-elegant sort of way, to serve to guests. Add a loaf of crusty bread, a class of Chianti Classico, and, for dessert, maybe some wine-poached pears and amaretti cookies.

1 pound spicy Italian sausage
3 tablespoons olive oil
1½ cups coarsely chopped onion
1 large red bell pepper, coarsely
    chopped
3 cups drained cooked white
    beans such as cannellini,
    rinsed

1 cup dry white wine
3 tablespoons chopped fresh
    thyme or 2 teaspoons dried
1 large bunch arugula

1) Cut the sausages in 3-inch lengths. Place them in a large skillet with a lid, add ¼ cup of water, and cook covered over low heat for 5 minutes. Uncover, raise the heat to medium, and cook until the sausages are browned outside and no longer pink in the center, 8 to 10 minutes. Remove to a plate and pour off all but 1 tablespoon of the pan drippings. (Keep the sausages warm in a low oven, or reheat in a microwave when ready to serve.)

2) Add the olive oil to the skillet. Add the onion and red pepper and cook over medium-high heat, stirring frequently, until slightly softened and browned, about 5 minutes. Add the beans, wine, and thyme, raise the heat to high, and cook until most of the wine is absorbed or reduced, 3 to 5 minutes.

3) Spread the arugula out on a platter. Spoon the warm beans over the greens. Slice the cooked sausages on a sharp diagonal and arrange over the beans. Serve immediately.

LOW COUNTRY HOPPIN' JOHN

6 main-dish servings

I*t's a long-standing tradition to serve Hoppin' John on New Year's Day in the South, but I love this comfortable dish at any time of year. Excellent quality frozen black-eyed peas are more and more available in supermarkets and are, in my opinion, far better than canned or even soaked and cooked dried peas. Fresh field peas are a rare treat, but if you happen to find yourself in South Carolina, they're well worth searching out.*

6 slices bacon (about 4 ounces), coarsely chopped
2 cups chopped onion
1 large rib celery with leaves, chopped
2 cloves garlic, finely chopped
2 (10-ounce) packages frozen black-eyed peas (see Note)
1 cup raw long-grain rice
1 bay leaf
¾ teaspoon salt, or to taste
½ teaspoon freshly ground pepper
½ teaspoon Tabasco, or to taste

CONDIMENTS
Chopped red onion, chopped tomatoes, olive oil, white wine vinegar

1) In a large, heavy saucepan, cook the bacon over medium-low heat until crisp and brown, 8 to 10 minutes. Remove bacon and drain on paper towels. Pour off all but 3 tablespoons of the fat.

2) Add the onion to the drippings and cook, stirring frequently, until it begins to soften, about 4 minutes. Add the celery and garlic and cook, stirring, for 1 minute.

3) Add 5 cups of water to the pan, along with the black-eyed peas, rice, bay leaf, salt, and pepper. Bring to a gentle boil, reduce the heat to low, and cook covered until the beans and rice are both tender, about 20 minutes. The result should be slightly more soupy than a regular rice dish. Discard the bay leaf.

4) Season with Tabasco. Serve the hoppin' John sprinkled with the reserved bacon and pass some or all of the suggested condiments at the table.

NOTE: Four cups drained, cooked black-eyed peas can substitute for the frozen peas.

CLASSIC TEXAS POT BEANS
WITH PICO DE GALLO

6 main-course servings;
8 to 10 side-dish servings

The mainstay meal of early cowboys, Texas pot beans are surrounded by almost as much lore as is Davy Crockett. One story has it that cowboys ate a few beans the first day they were cooked, a few more the second day, and by the third day, they were rubbing their bellies and saying they sure as hell wished they'd waited, 'cause the beans was just gettin' good! Pot beans do improve if allowed to "cure" for a day, and they do make a simple but magnificent meal, topped by pico de gallo (or "rooster's beak" salsa), and served with a basket of warm corn tortillas. Of course, pot beans can also be turned into "Never-Fried" Beans (page 64) or used in all kinds of other ways as a side dish.

POT BEANS

1 pound dried pinto beans, rinsed and picked over
2 ham hocks or 1 meaty ham bone
1 large onion, chopped
3 cloves garlic, chopped
2 jalapeño peppers, fresh or pickled, finely chopped
¾ teaspoon salt, or more as necessary
½ teaspoon freshly ground black pepper
½ teaspoon Tabasco

PICO DE GALLO SALSA

2 large, ripe tomatoes, seeded and chopped
1 cup chopped onion
1 small green bell pepper, seeded and chopped
2 jalapeño peppers, finely chopped
1 tablespoon lime juice
¼ cup chopped cilantro
¾ teaspoon salt
½ teaspoon sugar
¼ teaspoon Tabasco, or to taste

1) If you like, soak the beans in water to cover for 4 hours or overnight. Drain into a colander. In a large soup pot, bring 8 cups of water to a boil. Add the soaked or unsoaked beans, ham hocks, onion, garlic, jalapeños, and salt. Bring to a boil, reduce the heat to low, and cook covered until the beans are almost tender, 1½ to

2 hours. Remove as much meat as possible from the ham bones, cut into small dice, and return the meat to the pot. Discard the bones.

2) Simmer the beans uncovered until they are very tender and the liquid is thick, 30 to 60 minutes. They should still be somewhat soupy. Season with pepper and Tabasco and adjust the salt if necessary. (Can be made 3 days ahead or frozen. Reheat gently, adding a bit of additional liquid if too thick.)

3) For the salsa, combine the tomatoes, onion, green pepper, and jalapeño peppers in a bowl. Add the lime juice, cilantro, salt, sugar, and Tabasco. Let stand at room temperature for 15 minutes to blend flavors or refrigerate for up to 6 hours. Stir before serving.

4) Ladle the beans into shallow soup bowls and serve topped with the salsa.

SMOKY PORK AND PINTO BEAN CHILI WITH CHIPOTLES

8 servings

This fabulous chili is thickened and enriched with toasted pumpkin seeds and flavored with the smoky complexity of chipotle and ancho chiles. Brick-red chipotle peppers are dried, smoked jalapeños, and have recently become a favorite ingredient of "new American" chefs. They're very hot, but it's their smoky flavor, particularly when combined with ancho chiles, that adds a haunting depth to this dish. Chipotles are available both dried and canned and are well worth searching out.

3 dried chipotle chiles (see Note)
2 ancho chiles or 1 large dried New Mexican chile
1¼ cups pumpkin seeds
1 tablespoon vegetable oil
2 pounds ground pork
1 teaspoon salt
½ teaspoon freshly ground black pepper
2 cups chopped onion
5 cloves garlic, finely chopped
2 tablespoons ground cumin

1 (28-ounce) can crushed tomatoes
3 cups drained cooked pinto beans, rinsed
1 teaspoon sugar

ACCOMPANIMENTS AND GARNISHES
Rice, corn bread, reserved toasted pumpkin seeds, sour cream, chopped tomato, and chopped fresh jalapeño peppers (for those who like an extra hit of heat)

1) In a small bowl, soak the dried chiles in 2½ cups hot water until softened, about 30 minutes. Drain and reserve the soaking liquid.
2) Spread the pumpkin seeds out on a baking sheet and toast in a 350-degree oven until the seeds are fragrant and turn from green to light brown, 8 to 10 minutes. Watch carefully to prevent scorching. Measure out and reserve ½ cup of the seeds for garnish.
3) In a food processor purée the remaining ¾ cup of pumpkin seeds with the chiles and ½ cup of the soaking water. Reserve the remaining 2 cups of soaking liquid to use later in the chili.
4) In a large skillet or dutch oven, heat the vegetable oil over medium heat. Season the pork with salt and pepper and sauté, along

with the onion and garlic, stirring frequently, until the meat loses
its pink color, about 10 minutes. Stir in the cumin and cook, stirring,
for 1 minute.

5) Add the crushed tomatoes, pumpkin seed and chile purée,
remaining chile soaking liquid, beans, and sugar. Bring to a boil over
high heat, reduce the heat to medium-low, and simmer uncovered
for about 30 minutes, until slightly thickened. Taste for seasoning,
correcting if necessary. (Can be made 2 days ahead and refrigerated
or frozen. Reheat gently.)

6) Serve the chili with rice or with corn bread, and sprinkle it
with the reserved toasted pumpkin seeds, then top with any or all of
the other suggested garnishes.

NOTE: If you use canned chipotles, increase the number from
3 to 5. They're already rehydrated, so just purée with the soaked
New Mexican or ancho chiles.

CINCINNATI-STYLE CHILI
WITH FIXIN'S

6 to 8 servings **T**his concoction is an
*American phenomenon: a Mexican-style dish invented in a
city that has few Mexicans and now served in chili parlors
run mainly by Greeks. The spicy sauce can be ladled over hot
dogs, but if it's spooned over spaghetti and topped with kidney
beans, cheese, and onions, it's known as "five-way" chili. It
makes really terrific party fare, along with a big green salad.*

2 pounds ground beef
1½ cups chopped onion
3 cloves garlic, finely chopped
3 tablespoons chili powder
1 tablespoon paprika
1 teaspoon ground cumin
½ teaspoon ground allspice
½ teaspoon cayenne
2 cups beef broth
1 (16-ounce) can tomato sauce
2 tablespoons red wine vinegar
2 teaspoons Worcestershire
    sauce

1 bay leaf
1 cinnamon stick, broken in half
½ ounce unsweetened chocolate
Salt
Freshly ground black pepper
1 pound dried spaghetti
2 cups drained cooked kidney
    beans, rinsed
1½ cups grated sharp Cheddar
    cheese (6 ounces)
1 cup chopped white onion

1) In a large, deep skillet or saucepan, cook the meat, onion, and
garlic over medium heat, stirring occasionally, until the meat loses
its red color, about 10 minutes. Break up large clumps with the side
of a spoon. Spoon off any excess fat.

2) Add the chili powder, paprika, cumin, allspice, and cayenne, and
cook, stirring, for 1 minute. Stir in the beef broth, tomato sauce,
vinegar, Worcestershire, bay leaf, cinnamon stick, and chocolate.
Simmer uncovered over medium-low heat until the sauce thickens
and the flavors meld, 45 minutes to 1 hour. Stir occasionally to make
sure it doesn't scorch. The sauce should be moderately thick. Adjust
liquid if necessary. Season with salt and pepper to taste. Discard
the bay leaf. (Can be made 2 days ahead and refrigerated or frozen.
Reheat gently before serving.)

3) Cook the spaghetti in a large pot of boiling salted water until al dente, about 10 minutes. Drain in a colander.

4) Add a bit of water to the beans and heat gently in a saucepan or in a microwave.

5) To serve, ladle the sauce over the spaghetti. Pass the beans, cheese, and onion to sprinkle over the top.

TURKEY AND BLACK BEAN CHILI VERDE

4 servings

This very spicy black and green chili is nicely tamed when spooned over steamed rice and served with warmed corn tortillas. Some canned "mild" green chiles are hotter than others. This should be a spicy chili, so add a bit of Tabasco if you think it's lacking in heat. A salad of romaine lettuce with sliced oranges and red onions makes a pleasantly sweet/tart accompaniment.

2 tablespoons vegetable oil
1 pound ground turkey
¼ teaspoon freshly ground
    black pepper
2 cloves garlic, finely chopped
1½ tablespoons cornmeal
2 teaspoons ground cumin
1½ cups chopped scallions,
    including green tops

1½ cups reduced-sodium
    chicken broth
2 cups drained cooked black
    beans, rinsed
½ cup chopped mild green
    chiles (4-ounce can)
½ cup chopped fresh cilantro
Tabasco to taste, if necessary

1) Heat the vegetable oil in a large skillet or dutch oven. Season the turkey with black pepper and sauté over medium heat, stirring frequently, until the meat loses its pink color, 8 to 10 minutes. Add the garlic, cornmeal, and cumin and cook, stirring, for 1 minute. Add the scallions and cook, stirring, for 30 seconds.

2) Add the broth, beans, and chiles. Bring to a boil, reduce the heat to medium-low, and simmer uncovered until slightly reduced and thickened, about 15 minutes. (Can be made 2 days ahead and refrigerated or frozen. Reheat gently before finishing.)

3) Shortly before serving, stir in the cilantro and simmer for 1 minute. Taste for seasoning and add Tabasco if necessary.

CHICKEN CHILI BLANCO

4 servings

This is an interesting *"white" chili—a lovely oregano-flecked delicate beige color, with a creamy texture but a surprisingly zippy kick of peppery flavor. It's a perfect use for leftover cooked chicken or supermarket rotisserie-roasted chicken. Serve this splendid chili with steamed rice or rolled warm corn tortillas.*

1 tablespoon olive oil
1½ cups chopped onion
3 cloves garlic, finely chopped
2 teaspoons dried oregano
1½ teaspoons ground cumin
½ teaspoon powdered ginger
1½ cups chicken broth
½ cup dry white wine
1 bay leaf, broken in half
2 cups shredded cooked chicken
   (see Note)
2 cups drained cooked white
   beans, rinsed

2 jalapeño peppers, fresh or
   pickled, minced
1½ cups grated Monterey Jack
   cheese
½ teaspoon black pepper,
   preferably coarsely ground
Salt
4 cups cooked white or brown
   rice
GARNISHES
Diced tomatoes, chopped
   scallions, sliced black olives

1) Heat the olive oil in a large saucepan. Add the onion and sauté over medium heat until softened and lightly browned, 5 to 8 minutes. Add the garlic, oregano, cumin, and ginger and cook, stirring, for 1 minute. Add the broth, wine, and bay leaf. Cook uncovered over medium-high heat until somewhat reduced, 5 to 8 minutes.

2) Add the chicken, beans, and jalapeños. Simmer uncovered for 10 minutes, stirring occasionally. Using the back of a spoon, mash about one quarter of the beans to thicken the sauce. (Can be made 2 days ahead and refrigerated, or frozen. Reheat gently before finishing.)

3) Over low heat, add the cheese one handful at a time, stirring until melted. Add the pepper and salt to taste.

4) Remove the pieces of bay leaf. Serve the chili topped with some or all of the garnishes.

NOTE: You can substitute uncooked skinless, boneless chicken breast or thigh meat. Cut in ¾-inch dice and add with the broth in Step 1.

STREAMLINED BRAZILIAN FEIJOADA
WITH ACCOMPANIMENTS

8 to 10 servings

This smoked meat and black bean stew is the national dish of Brazil. In its most classic and elaborate form it uses such exotica as corned spareribs, pork knuckle, and carne seca, a type of dried, salted meat that is a specialty in Brazil. My version simplifies and updates this succulent dish, while at the same time remaining true to the spirit of the original. Feijoada and its accompaniments make one of those fabulous feast dishes that demands to be shared with friends in an atmosphere of fun and laughter. So put on some Brazilian samba music, set a colorful, festive table, and have a party!

FEIJOADA

1 pound dried black beans, rinsed and picked over

2 cups chopped onion

1½ cups chopped celery

4 cloves garlic, chopped

1 bay leaf

¼ pound bacon, preferably slab bacon, diced

12 ounces chorizo or kielbasa, cut in ¾-inch slices

1½ pounds lean boneless pork, cubed

12 ounces smoked ham, diced

1 (28-ounce) can plum tomatoes, drained and chopped

3 cups raw long-grain rice cooked in 6 cups salted water

2 (10-ounce) packages frozen collard greens, cooked according to package directions and drained

4 seedless oranges, peeled and diced

PEPPER AND LIME SAUCE

3 large tomatoes, seeded and chopped

1½ cups chopped red onion

3 pickled Tabasco or jalapeño peppers or 1 Scotch bonnet pepper, minced (see Note)

½ cup lime juice

¼ cup olive oil

1) If you like, soak the beans in water to cover for 4 hours or overnight. Drain into a colander. In a large soup pot, bring 8 cups of water to a boil. Add the soaked or unsoaked beans, onion, celery, garlic, and bay leaf. Bring to a boil, reduce the heat to low, and cook covered for 1 hour.

2) Meanwhile, in a large sauté pan, cook the bacon and sausage over medium heat, stirring frequently, until browned. Remove with a slotted spoon to a plate, leaving the drippings in the pan. Add the pork and ham and cook, stirring frequently, until browned.

3) Add the meats to the bean pot and continue cooking until the beans are tender, 1 to 2 hours. Add the tomatoes and simmer for 15 minutes. The beans should be thick but somewhat soupy. Discard the bay leaf. (Can be made 2 days ahead and refrigerated, or frozen. Reheat gently, adding a bit more liquid to thin if necessary.)

4) For the pepper and lime sauce, combine the tomatoes, onion, and hot peppers in a bowl. Add the lime juice and olive oil and set aside so flavors can blend for at least 1 hour. (Can be made several hours ahead and refrigerated.)

5) Serve the feijoada from a large bowl, with the rice, collards, diced oranges, and pepper and lime sauce on the side.

NOTE: Tabasco peppers are small, hot red peppers that are available pickled—usually in a tall, narrow jar—in Spanish markets and in supermarkets that sell a line of Spanish products.

CASSOULET WITH HERBED PEPPER CRUMB CRUST

8 to 10 servings

My version of cassoulet *is somewhat simplified and pared down to suit modern appetites, but is nevertheless so meltingly succulent that it could become your favorite dinner party dish of all time. I strongly urge you to look for fresh herbs to use in the cassoulet, for they seem to me to make all the difference in lifting and lightening the innate richness of this marvelous classic.*

WHITE BEANS

1 pound dried white beans such as Great Northern or navy beans, rinsed and picked over (see Note)

1 large smoked ham hock

1 large onion, coarsely chopped

3 cloves garlic, peeled and crushed

6 sprigs fresh thyme or 1 teaspoon dried thyme

2 bay leaves

MEATS AND ASSEMBLY

1 duck (4 pounds), cut in 8 pieces

½ teaspoon freshly ground black pepper

1 pound kielbasa or chorizo or other garlicky smoked sausage, sliced in 1-inch pieces

1 pound lean lamb, cut in 2-inch cubes

2 cups sliced onion

4 cloves garlic, chopped

2 cups dry white wine

1 tablespoon chopped fresh rosemary or 1½ teaspoons crumbled dried rosemary

1 tablespoon chopped fresh thyme or 2 teaspoons dried thyme

2 cups beef or chicken broth

1 (16-ounce) can chopped tomatoes with juice

Salt

HERBED PEPPER CRUMBS

2½ cups fresh bread crumbs made from day-old French bread

¼ cup chopped parsley

1½ tablespoons chopped fresh rosemary or 2 teaspoons crumbled dried rosemary

1½ tablespoons chopped fresh thyme or 2 teaspoons dried thyme

1 teaspoon freshly ground black pepper

2 tablespoons olive oil

1) If you like, soak the beans in water to cover for 4 hours or overnight. Drain into a colander. In a large soup pot, bring 12 cups of water to a boil. Add the soaked or unsoaked beans, ham hock, onion, garlic, thyme, and bay leaves. Cover, reduce the heat to very low, and simmer until the beans are tender but not mushy, 1½ to 2 hours. Discard the ham hock, thyme sprigs, and bay leaves.

2) Sprinkle the duck pieces with pepper. Heat a large covered skillet or dutch oven over medium heat, arrange the duck pieces skin side down in the pan, and cook until some of the fat renders and the duck is deep golden brown, 15 to 20 minutes. Remove to a plate and pour off all but ¼ cup of the drippings.

3) Add the sausage and lamb to the pan drippings and cook until nicely browned on all sides, about 10 minutes. Remove to the plate with the duck, leaving the drippings in the pan.

4) Cook the onion in the drippings, stirring occasionally, until softened, about 5 minutes. Add the garlic and cook, stirring, for 1 minute. Add the wine, raise the heat to high, and cook, stirring up the browned bits on the bottom of the pan, until slightly reduced, about 3 minutes.

5) Return the meat and accumulated juices to the pan. Add the rosemary, thyme, broth, and tomatoes. Cook covered over medium-low heat until the duck meat is no longer pink, about 30 minutes. Spoon off excess fat. (Or, refrigerate, and when cold,the fat can be lifted off the top.)

6) Transfer the meat mixture to a 4-quart casserole or two smaller baking dishes. Drain the beans, reserving the liquid. Add the beans to the meat mixture, stirring gently so as not to crush them, and add enough reserved bean liquid to come to the top of the solids. Taste, seasoning with salt if necessary. (Can be prepared 2 days ahead and refrigerated. Return to room temperature before baking, adding a bit more broth or water if all the liquid has been absorbed. The cassoulet should be somewhat soupy when it goes into the oven.)

7) For the crumbs, toss the bread crumbs with the parsley, rosemary, thyme, and pepper. Drizzle with the olive oil and toss until well combined.

8) Preheat the oven to 350 degrees.

9) Sprinkle the casserole(s) with the crumbs and bake uncovered in the center of the preheated oven until most of the juices are absorbed and the top is crusty and golden brown, 1 to 1½ hours.

10) Serve hot, directly from the baking dish.

NOTE: Canned bean option: In a large saucepan, sauté 2 cups chopped onion and 2 cloves garlic in 2 tablespoons olive oil until softened. Add 4 cups chicken broth, 1 teaspoon dried thyme, and 6 cups rinsed and drained cooked white beans. Simmer, covered, for 15 minutes. Use beans and broth as you would in Step 6 of the main recipe. For the duck, ask the butcher or supermarket meat manager to cut the bird into 8 sections.

LAMB AND WHITE BEAN STEW
À LA BRETONNE

4 servings

This is a simplified version of a famous lamb and white bean dish from Brittany. The renowned pré-salé lamb from that French region has a subtly salty tang because the sheep spend their short lives happily grazing on the wind-swept salt marshes. White beans and lamb make a succulent combination, with the intense flavor of the meat (and the garlic) playing off the neutrality of the beans. Serve the stew with crusty peasant bread, a salad of dark bitter greens, such as escarole, and a glass of red wine.

1 pound lean, boneless lamb,
    cut in 2-inch cubes
½ teaspoon salt
½ teaspoon freshly ground
    pepper
2 tablespoons unsalted butter
4 cloves garlic, finely chopped
1 tablespoon crumbled dried
    rosemary or 1½ tablespoons
    fresh

1 cup dry white wine
3 cups drained cooked white
    beans such as cannellini,
    rinsed
2 (14- to 16-ounce) cans
    chopped stewed tomatoes

1) Season the lamb with salt and pepper. In a large skillet, heat the butter. Sauté the lamb over medium heat, turning frequently, until the meat is browned on all sides, about 6 minutes. Add the garlic and rosemary and cook, stirring, for 1 minute.

2) Add the wine and bring to a boil over high heat, stirring up any browned bits clinging to the pan. Add the beans and tomatoes and simmer the stew uncovered over medium-low heat until the meat is no longer pink in the center and the sauce is somewhat reduced and thickened, about 25 minutes.

3) Taste the stew for seasoning, adding more salt and pepper as necessary, and serve.

BURGUNDY STREET
RED BEANS 'N' RICE

6 servings

My first taste of red beans 'n' rice in New Orleans was one of those eating epiphanies. It was at Buster Holmes's very simple but very atmospheric storefront cafe on Burgundy Street, where all the food was cooked in a tiny kitchen in the back. This is straightforward soulful New Orleans–style comfort food at its best, and when I make this warming dish on a chilly Sunday afternoon I am instantly transported back to that day in "the Big Easy."

1½ cups (about 12 ounces) dried red beans or kidney beans, rinsed and picked over (see Note)
1 meaty ham bone or 2 ham hocks
1 tablespoon olive oil
12 ounces andouille or other spicy smoked sausage such as kielbasa, cut in 1-inch slices
1½ cups chopped onion
1 large green bell pepper, chopped
1 stalk celery, chopped
4 scallions, including green tops, sliced
2 bay leaves
1 teaspoon dried thyme
¼ teaspoon freshly ground black pepper
1½ cups raw long-grain rice
1 teaspoon salt
½ teaspoon Tabasco

1) If you like, soak the beans in water to cover for 4 hours or overnight. Drain into a colander. In a large soup pot, bring 6 cups of water to a boil. Add the soaked or unsoaked beans and ham bone, bring to a boil, and reduce the heat to low. Cook covered until the beans are almost but not quite tender, 1 to 1½ hours. Remove the ham bone(s) with tongs and, when cool enough to handle, cut any meat off the bone and add to the beans. Discard the bone.
2) In a large skillet, heat the olive oil over medium heat. Add the sausage and cook, stirring frequently, until it begins to brown, about 5 minutes. Add the onion, bell pepper, celery, and scallions. Cook, stirring frequently, until the vegetables begin to soften, about 5 minutes. Scrape the sausage/vegetable mixture into the pot with the beans.

3) Add the bay leaves, thyme, and black pepper to the pot and continue cooking uncovered over low heat until the beans are very tender, 30 to 45 minutes. (Can be made 2 days ahead to this point. Cover and refrigerate. Reheat gently before proceeding.)

4) Meanwhile, bring 3 cups of water to a boil in a medium-large saucepan. Add the rice and salt, stir once, and cook covered over very low heat until the rice is tender and the liquid is absorbed, about 20 minutes.

5) Using the back of a spoon, mash about a fourth of the beans against the side of the pan to thicken the mixture. Season with Tabasco and taste for salt. (The beans will probably not need any because the smoked meats are quite salty.) Discard the bay leaves. Add a bit more liquid if necessary. The beans should be thick but soupy enough to be ladled out.

6) To serve, spoon the red beans over the hot cooked rice.

NOTE: Canned bean option: You can substitute 4 cups of rinsed and drained canned cooked beans for the dried beans. Simmer them with about 3 cups of water along with the sausage and vegetables.

NEW ENGLAND "FROM SCRATCH" BAKED BEANS

6 to 8 main-dish servings; more side-dish servings

These beans are very close to the ones served at the baked bean suppers in the area of coastal Maine where I spend summers, although the dried bean of choice in that vicinity is a spotted beauty called the Jacob's Cattle bean. Local women donate all the food for these family-style summertime fund-raising suppers, and the menu, in addition to the slightly (but not overly) sweet "from scratch" beans, includes fragrant steamed brown bread, yeasty dinner rolls, coleslaw, crisp half-sour pickles, and some of the best homemade pies this side of paradise.

1 pound dried small white beans such as navy or Great Northern, rinsed and picked over (see Note)
½ teaspoon salt, approximately (more if not using salt pork)
1 cup chopped onion
2 teaspoons dried mustard

1 teaspoon powdered ginger
½ teaspoon freshly ground black pepper
¼ cup cider vinegar
¼ cup molasses
¼ cup maple syrup
¼ pound lean salt pork (optional)

1) If you like, soak the beans in water to cover for 4 hours or overnight. Drain into a colander. In a large soup pot, bring 8 cups of water to a boil. Add the soaked or unsoaked beans and salt, bring to a boil, and reduce the heat to low. Cook covered until the beans are just tender, 1½ to 2 hours. Drain.

2) Preheat the oven to 325 degrees.

3) In a 2½- to 3-quart casserole, combine the onion, mustard, ginger, and pepper. Add the vinegar, molasses, and maple syrup, and stir to combine. Add the drained beans and enough water to cover the beans by about ½ inch. Score the fat on the salt pork, if using, and insert fat side up in the beans.

4) Cover the casserole and bake for 4 hours. Check about every hour, and if the liquid has cooked away, add enough boiling water to keep the beans slightly soupy at all times.

5) Uncover, and cook for a final 30 minutes or until the sauce thickens and the salt pork browns.

NOTE: Canned bean option: You can use 6 cups of drained cooked white beans instead of cooking dried beans, if you like. For a vegetarian option, omit the salt pork and use vegetable broth for the liquid.

QUICK SWEET AND SOUR
BEAN BAKE

4 main course servings;
6 to 8 side-dish servings

If I'm short of time, sometimes I take these deliciously doctored-up shortcut baked beans to potluck suppers. I don't always mention that they're not exactly "from scratch," and no one has objected yet. You can double or triple the recipe, using the extra-large cans of beans, and you'll probably find that whatever the amount, the dish will be scraped clean!

1 tablespoon vegetable oil
1½ cups chopped onion
1 small green bell pepper, seeded and finely chopped
2 teaspoons dry mustard
½ cup packed brown sugar
3 tablespoons cider vinegar
2 tablespoons ketchup
¼ teaspoon cinnamon
3 (15- to 16-ounce) cans (or the equivalent) pork and beans with sauce
4 bacon slices, cut in half to make 8 pieces

1) Preheat the oven to 350 degrees.

2) In a large skillet, heat the vegetable oil. Add the onion and cook over medium heat, stirring frequently, until it begins to soften, about 4 minutes. Add the green pepper and cook, stirring, until it begins to soften, about 3 minutes. Add the dry mustard and cook, stirring, for 1 minute. Stir in the brown sugar, vinegar, ketchup, and cinnamon. Add the beans, stirring to combine well.

3) Transfer the bean mixture to a 2-quart baking dish. Cover with foil and bake in the preheated oven for 30 minutes.

4) Remove the foil and arrange the bacon pieces over the bean mixture. Return to the oven and bake uncovered until the sauce reduces and the bacon browns and crisps, 45 to 50 minutes. (The beans can be baked several hours ahead and refrigerated. Reheat the covered casserole at 350 degrees until hot and bubbly, adding a bit of water if necessary.)

PORK IN BLACK BEAN SAUCE ON ASIAN NOODLES

3 to 4 servings

Bottled black bean sauce is available in Asian markets and by now in many supermarkets. It is one of those staple Chinese sauces that keeps for months in the refrigerator, just waiting for your yen for a simple and satisfying Asian dish. The black bean sauce is made with preserved beans puréed with an array of such delectable seasonings as ginger, sesame, sherry, and garlic.

Salt
12 ounces fresh Asian noodles
    or fresh egg pasta, or
    8 ounces dried pasta such
    as vermicelli
1 tablespoon peanut or
    vegetable oil
12 ounces lean, boneless pork,
    cut in thin crosswise slices
½ teaspoon freshly ground
    black pepper
¼ cup black bean sauce

1 tablespoon reduced-sodium
    soy sauce
1 tablespoon sesame oil
2 teaspoons rice wine vinegar
2 teaspoons sugar
½ cup chopped honey-roasted
    peanuts
⅓ cup thinly sliced scallions,
    including green tops
3 tablespoons chopped fresh
    cilantro

1) Bring a large pot of salted water to a boil. Add noodles or other pasta and cook uncovered at a rapid boil until al dente, about 4 minutes for fresh noodles, about 10 minutes for dry pasta. Drain in a colander, reserving ⅓ cup of the cooking water. Transfer to a warm serving platter.

2) Meanwhile, heat the peanut or vegetable oil in a large skillet or wok. Season the pork with black pepper and stir-fry over medium-high heat until browned on all sides, about 2 minutes. Reduce the heat to low, add the black bean sauce, soy sauce, sesame oil, vinegar, sugar, and the ⅓ cup of pasta cooking water. Bring to a simmer, stirring until sugar dissolves.

3) Spoon sauce over cooked noodles and sprinkle with peanuts, scallions, and cilantro.

MISSION BEAN AND TURKEY ENCHILADAS

4 servings

Leftover cooked turkey or chicken is put to excellent use in these simple and very satisfying enchiladas. Watch out for the jalapeño-studded Jack cheese! I love it, but it is quite amazingly hot, so if you prefer, use regular Jack and add your own judicious amount of chopped jalapeños.

1 (14- to 16-ounce) can Mexican-style stewed tomatoes

1 cup loosely packed cilantro sprigs

1 teaspoon ground cumin

1 (10-ounce) can enchilada sauce (see Note)

2 cups grated Monterey Jack cheese with jalapeños

1 cup drained cooked pinto beans, rinsed

1 cup (4 ounces) diced cooked turkey or chicken

8 (6-inch) corn tortillas

Shredded iceberg or romaine lettuce

Sliced black olives

Sliced scallions

1) In a food processor, combine the stewed tomatoes, cilantro, and cumin. Pulse to make a fairly smooth purée. Transfer the purée to a saucepan, add the enchilada sauce, and cook over medium heat until warm, about 2 minutes.

2) In a mixing bowl, combine 1 cup of the cheese with the beans and turkey. Toss to mix well.

3) Spoon about 1 cup of the sauce into the bottom of a 7- by 11-inch baking dish.

4) Dip a tortilla in the warm sauce to soften; then place flat on a work surface and fill with one-eighth of the filling mixture. Roll to enclose the filling and place seam side down in the baking dish. Repeat with the remaining tortillas and filling, placing the enchiladas close together in the dish. Pour the remaining sauce over the enchiladas and sprinkle with the remaining 1 cup of cheese. (Can be made several hours ahead. Cover with foil and refrigerate.)

5) Preheat the oven to 450 degrees. If the casserole has not been refrigerated, bake uncovered until the cheese melts and the sauce is bubbly, 10 to 15 minutes. If made ahead, bake with the foil on until heated through, 20 to 25 minutes.

6) Serve hot directly from the baking dish. Pass the lettuce, olives, and scallions at the table.

NOTE: If you can't get canned enchilada sauce, substitute an 8-ounce can of tomato sauce and 3 tablespoons of hot salsa.

MOROCCAN CHICKEN AND VEGETABLE COUSCOUS

8 to 10 servings

Couscous with all the trimmings (albeit in modernized, streamlined form) makes a wonderfuly festive and exotic party dish. Don't be daunted by the long ingredients list. All except for the "cooking" of the couscous grain itself is done in one large pot and can be made well ahead. The traditional accompanying sauce in Morocco is harissa, an extremely hot dried red pepper paste that gets mixed with a bit of the cooking broth and served as a condiment over the couscous. Harissa can be puchased in some specialty stores, but if you can't find it, this recipe for hot pepper paste makes an excellent substitute.

3 tablespoons olive oil
1¾ pounds boneless chicken thighs or breasts, cut in rough 2-inch pieces
¾ teaspoon salt
½ teaspoon cayenne
2 cups chopped onion
4 cloves garlic, finely chopped
2 teaspoons ground cumin
1 teaspoon curry powder
6 cups chicken broth
2 cinnamon sticks, broken in half
8 slender carrots, peeled and cut in 2-inch lengths

12 ounces white turnips, peeled and cut in rough 2-inch chunks
2 cups drained cooked chick-peas, rinsed
3 small, slender zucchini, cut in 1-inch lengths
1 large red bell pepper, seeded, cut in rough 2-inch dice
1½ cups pitted prunes
1 cup golden raisins
12 cups cooked couscous (see Note)
⅓ cup purchased harissa *or* Hot Pepper Paste (recipe follows)

1) Heat the olive oil over medium-high heat in a very large covered pan or dutch overn. Sprinkle the chicken with the salt and cayenne and sauté in the oil until browned, about 5 minutes. Remove with tongs or a slotted spoon to a plate, leaving the drippings in the pan.
2) Add the onion and cook, stirring occasionally, until it begins to soften, about 4 minutes. Add the garlic, cumin, and curry powder and cook, stirring, for 1 minute.

3) Add the broth, cinnamon sticks, carrots, and turnips. Bring to a boil over high heat, reduce the heat to low, and cook covered for 10 minutes.

4) Add the chick-peas, zucchini, red pepper, prunes, and raisins. Return the chicken to the stew and simmer over medium-low heat, partially covered, until the vegetables are tender and the chicken is cooked through, about 20 minutes. Taste for seasoning, correcting if necessary. (Can be made several hours ahead and refrigerated. Reheat gently.) Measure out ½ cup of broth and set aside.

5) To serve, mound couscous on a large, rimmed platter or on individual rimmed plates or in shallow soup bowls. Spoon chicken and vegetables around couscous and ladle broth over.

6) Stir the ½ cup of reserved broth into the harissa or hot pepper paste and pass at the table.

NOTE: For the couscous, bring 4½ cups water to a boil in a large saucepan. Add 2 teaspoons salt and stir in 2 (10-ounce) packages (3 cups) couscous. Cover, remove from the heat, and let stand 5 to 6 minutes until liquid is absorbed and couscous softens. Fluff with a fork before serving.

HOT PEPPER PASTE

About ⅓ cup

2 tablespoons dried red pepper flakes	¾ teaspoon salt
	3 tablespoons boiling water
1 teaspoon ground coriander seed	1½ tablespoons olive oil
	2 cloves garlic, minced
1 teaspoon ground cumin	

In a small bowl, combine the red pepper flakes, coriander, cumin, and salt. Pour boiling water over and stir to combine. Stir in the olive oil and garlic. Set the mixture aside to steep at room temperature for 1 hour or refrigerate for several days. Return to room temperature before adding broth and serving.

BROILED SEA BASS ON GREEN LENTIL SALAD

4 servings

In this dish, which is inspired by something similar served in a wonderful New York restaurant, fish fillets are marinated in spiced yogurt, broiled, and placed atop a bed of lemony and minted green lentils. Black sea bass fillets have a tender, delicate flesh that's really appealing, but if you can't get sea bass, substitute any other white, firm-fleshed thick fillets or steaks such as halibut, cod, or snapper.

YOGURT MARINADE

¼ cup plain yogurt
1 tablespoon Dijon mustard
1 teaspoon ground cumin
½ teaspoon ground coriander seed
¼ teaspoon cayenne
¼ teaspoon salt

~~~

4 fillets of sea bass, 4 to 6 ounces each

LENTILS

1 cup French green lentils, rinsed and picked over (see Note)
2 cups vegetable or chicken broth
3 tablespoons lemon juice
2 tablespoons olive oil
1 clove garlic, minced
3 tablespoons chopped fresh mint
¼ teaspoon freshly ground black pepper
Salt

1) In a shallow dish, combine the yogurt with the mustard, cumin, coriander, cayenne, and salt. Add the fish to the marinade, turning to coat all sides. Set aside at room temperature for 15 minutes or refrigerate up to 3 hours.

2) Combine the lentils and broth in a medium-sized saucepan. Bring to a boil, reduce the heat to low, and cook covered until the lentils are tender but not mushy, 35 to 45 minutes. Drain off any unabsorbed liquid and transfer to a bowl.

3) In a small bowl whisk together the lemon juice, olive oil, garlic, mint, and pepper. Pour over the warm lentils, toss gently, and season to taste with salt. (Rewarm over low heat or in a microwave if necessary before serving.)

4) Preheat the broiler. Arrange the fish on a broiler pan and cook 4 to 5 inches from the heat source until the fillets are flecked with brown on top and opaque but still moist within, 8 to 10 minutes, depending on the thickness of the fish.

5) Spoon a bed of warm lentils on each plate and top each serving with a piece of fish.

NOTE: Brown lentils work fine, too. They usually take 10 to 15 minutes less than green lentils to cook, so check for tenderness after about 25 minutes.

SHELLFISH AND WHITE BEAN STEW WITH CABBAGE

3 to 4 servings

A *few years ago, innovative chefs started experimenting with seafood and bean combinations. This marriage turns out to be a very successful one, and, as a bonus, many of the recipes (including this one) are also quite low in fat. This dish is a lot like a fabulous shellfish and white bean stew that I ate at Gramercy Tavern, a lovely New York restaurant. Serve it with crusty bread, a salad of sharp greens, and a clean red wine.*

2 tablespoons olive oil
1 leek, white and pale green parts only, washed and thinly sliced
2 cloves garlic, finely chopped
2 cups reduced-sodium chicken broth
1 cup clam juice
1 bay leaf
3 cups thinly sliced savoy cabbage

2 cups drained cooked white beans such as cannellini, rinsed
2 carrots, peeled and thinly sliced
1 tablespoon chopped fresh thyme or 1 teaspoon dried
8 jumbo shrimp
12 sea scallops
¼ cup chopped Italian parsley
White pepper
Salt

1) Heat the olive oil in a large, covered skillet or dutch oven. Add the leek and garlic and cook over medium heat, stirring frequently, for 5 minutes, until softened. Add the chicken broth, clam juice, and bay leaf. Cook uncovered over medium heat for about 5 minutes, until the liquid is slightly reduced.

2) Add the cabbage, beans, carrots, and thyme. Cook covered over low heat until the cabbage wilts and the carrots are tender, about 10 minutes. Discard the bay leaf. (Can be made 1 day ahead and refrigerated. Reheat gently before proceeding.)

3) Add the shrimp and scallops to the stew and cook covered until the shrimp turn pink and the scallops are opaque, about 5 minutes.

4) Add the parsley and heat through. Season the stew with pepper and salt, if necessary. Ladle into shallow bowls to serve.

BEAN MEATLESS MAIN DISHES

All recipes in this chapter are vegetarian.

ORECCHIETTE WITH BROCCOLI RABE AND WHITE BEANS

5 to 6 servings

Orecchiette, or "little ears," is the traditional pasta shape for this wonderful southern Italian dish. Use all of the broccoli rabe — flowers, leaves, and stems — and serve the pasta with a salad of sliced tomatoes drizzled with balsamic vinegar.

12 ounces orecchiette or other large, stubby pasta such as radiatore or penne
1 bunch broccoli rabe (1 to 1½ pounds), chopped in approximate 1½-inch lengths
¼ cup olive oil, preferably extra-virgin
6 cloves garlic, finely chopped
2 cups dry white wine
3 cups drained cooked cannellini or other white beans, rinsed
½ cup grated Parmesan cheese, preferably imported
Freshly ground black pepper
Salt

1) In a large pot of boiling salted water cook the orecchiette until almost al dente, about 9 minutes. Add the broccoli rabe to the pasta and cook another 2 to 3 minutes until the pasta is al dente and the broccoli rabe is crisp-tender. Drain into a colander.

2) Meanwhile, heat the olive oil in a large skillet and sauté the garlic over medium-low heat for 1 minute. Stir in the wine and beans. Simmer uncovered over medium heat for about 10 minutes until slightly reduced.

3) Toss the pasta and broccoli rabe with the sauce, add the cheese, season generously with pepper and with salt if necessary, and toss again.

SIMPLIFIED RISOTTO WITH PINK BEANS, ROASTED GARLIC, AND TOMATOES

3 to 4 servings

Make this dish at the height of summer when the markets and gardens are bursting with fragrant basil and meaty, ripe tomatoes. The beans contribute welcome body and texture to this risotto, and the roasted garlic adds a sophisticated finesse that lifts this into the "for company" category. You'll note that this recipe does not demand constant stirring while the rice cooks. I've followed the recommendation of Bon Appétit magazine's test kitchen, which experimented with both the classic and nontraditional methods, finding that this simplified version produces results that are virtually indistinguishable from the original. So, unless you really love to stand over a hot stove stirring rice for 20 minutes, give this a try. The result is exceptional!

6 cloves garlic, unpeeled
2½ tablespoons olive oil
4 cups vegetable broth
1¼ cups dry white wine
1 cup arborio rice
1½ cups drained cooked pink, red, or kidney beans, rinsed

½ cup grated Parmesan cheese
2 cups seeded, chopped tomatoes (about 12 ounces)
⅔ cup slivered fresh basil
¼ teaspoon freshly ground pepper
Salt

1) Preheat the oven to 400 degrees. Place the garlic cloves on a small sheet of foil, drizzle with ½ tablespoon of the olive oil, and wrap loosely. Roast in the preheated oven for about 30 minutes or until the garlic feels soft when the skin is pierced with a sharp knife point.

2) Meanwhile, combine the broth and wine in a saucepan and heat gently.

3) Heat the remaining 2 tablespoons of olive oil over medium to medium-high heat in a large, heavy saucepan. Add the rice and cook, stirring, until the grains are translucent and coated with oil, about

2 minutes. Ladle all but about ½ cup of the broth/wine mixture over the rice. Simmer uncovered, stirring every 4 to 5 minutes, until the rice is swollen, almost tender, and creamy, but still is slightly firm to the bite, about 18 minutes. Stir in the beans and remaining broth and heat through, about 2 minutes.

4) Squeeze the roasted garlic out of its skins and mash with a fork. Stir it into the risotto along with the cheese. Fold in the tomatoes and basil and season with pepper and salt to taste. If the risotto has absorbed all of its liquid, stir in a bit more hot broth or water. It should be neither soupy nor firm, but somewhere in between.

5) Serve the risotto in shallow soup bowls.

SPICED INDIAN RICE WITH PEAS

4 main-course servings;
6 to 8 side-dish servings

Fragrant Indian spices *perfume this absolutely delectable dish of rice and green peas. The basmati or Texmati rice contributes its own distinctively exotic note, but if it's not available, regular long-grain rice works just fine, too. I usually serve this as a meatless entrée, with condiments such as chutney and plain yogurt in addition to the toasted nuts, but it also makes a spectacular side dish to grilled lamb or chicken.*

3 tablespoons vegetable oil
1½ cups chopped onion
2 cloves garlic, finely chopped
1 tablespoon minced or grated
   fresh ginger
2 cups basmati or Texmati rice
1 tablespoon garam masala
   (see Note)
4 cups vegetable broth

¾ cup thinly sliced carrots
   (2 to 3 carrots)
¾ cup green beans, cut in
   ½-inch lengths (3 to 4 ounces)
1 cinnamon stick, broken in half
½ teaspoon salt, or more to
   taste
2 cups frozen peas
1 cup sliced almonds

1) In a large, covered skillet or dutch oven, heat the vegetable oil. Sauté the onion over medium heat, stirring frequently, until it softens and browns lightly, about 8 minutes. Add the garlic and ginger and cook for 1 minute. Add the rice and garam masala (or spices, see Note), and cook, stirring, until the rice is coated with oil and the spices are fragrant, about 2 minutes.

2) Add the broth, carrots, beans, cinnamon stick, and salt. Bring to a boil over high heat, reduce the heat to low, and cook covered for 15 minutes.

3) Add the peas, stir in gently with a fork, and cook until the rice is tender, about 5 minutes longer. Taste and season with additional salt if necessary.

4) Meanwhile, toast the almonds in a small skillet over medium heat, stirring frequently, until they turn pale gold and fragrant, 3 to 5 minutes.

5) Serve the rice sprinkled with the almonds.

NOTE: Garam masala is an Indian spice mixture sold in jars in specialty stores and many supermarkets. If you can't find it, substitute ¾ teaspoon ground cardamom seed, ¾ teaspoon ground coriander seed, ¾ teaspoon ground cumin, ½ teaspoon cayenne, and ¼ teaspoon ground cloves.

HERBED GREEN LENTILS ON PARMESAN POTATO PURÉE

4 servings

Tiny, flint green lentils are produced in the volcanic soil around the town of Le Puy in Auvergne, France. Their unique color, pleasantly firm texture, and light, fresh taste make them well worth seeking out in specialty food stores. Of course, the more commonly found brown lentils will work just fine in this dish, too — though if you do use them, count on a few minutes shorter cooking time. When I make the accompanying Parmesan potato purée, I like to leave some of the potato skins on for added texture and flavor.

HERBED GREEN LENTILS
2 tablespoons olive oil, preferably extra-virgin
½ cup chopped onion
1 large carrot, chopped
1 large rib celery, chopped
1 large clove garlic, chopped
4 to 5 cups vegetable broth
1½ cups green lentils, rinsed and picked over
1 (14- to 16-ounce) can stewed tomatoes with juice
1½ teaspoons chopped fresh sage or ½ teaspoon crumbled dried leaf sage
1 teaspoon chopped fresh rosemary or ½ teaspoon crumbled dried rosemary
1 bay leaf, broken in half
½ teaspoon salt, or to taste
¼ teaspoon freshly ground pepper
2 teaspoons balsamic vinegar

PARMESAN POTATO PURÉE
2 pounds russet or all-purpose potatoes
⅔ cup milk
¼ cup Parmesan cheese
2 tablespoons olive oil
¼ teaspoon freshly ground pepper
Salt

1) To make the lentils, heat the olive oil in a medium-sized saucepan. Add the onion, carrot, celery, and garlic and cook over medium heat, stirring frequently, until somewhat softened, about 8 minutes. Add 4 cups of the broth along with the lentils, tomatoes, sage, rosemary, bay leaf, salt, and pepper. Bring to a boil and cook covered over low heat until the lentils are tender but still hold their shape, 35 to 45 minutes. The lentils should be just slightly soupy. If they seem a bit dry, add the additional cup of broth. (Can be made 3 days ahead and refrigerated. Reheat before serving, adding a bit more liquid if necessary.)

2) For the Parmesan potato purée, partially or completely peel the potatoes, cut into rough 2½-inch chunks, and cook in lightly salted water to cover until tender when pierced with a sharp knife, 15 to 20 minutes. Drain, add the milk, Parmesan, and olive oil to the pan, and mash with a potato masher or beat with a wooden spoon to a not-completely-smooth purée. Season with pepper and salt to taste. (Since the Parmesan is salty, you may not need additional salt.)

3) Stir the vinegar into the lentils and discard the bay leaf. To serve, spoon lentils over or alongside the hot potato purée.

CUMIN-SCENTED EGGPLANT, CHICK-PEA, AND TOMATO RAGOUT

6 servings

Spiced with the irresistibly fragrant (and quite hot!) flavors of the Middle East, this stew is one of those dishes that I find myself craving every now and then. I like it best served over nutty, steamed couscous, perhaps with a cucumber salad on the side.

1 medium eggplant, about 1 to
   1¼ pounds
1 teaspoon salt, plus additional
   if necessary
3 tablespoons olive oil
2 cups chopped onion
1 green bell pepper, seeded and
   coarsely chopped
3 cloves garlic, chopped
1 tablespoon ground cumin
1½ teaspoons cinnamon
1 teaspoon ground ginger

1 teaspoon ground coriander
   seed
¼ teaspoon cayenne, or to taste
1¾ pounds ripe tomatoes,
   seeded and coarsely chopped
   or 2 (14- to 16-ounce) cans
   chopped tomatoes
2 cups drained cooked chick-
   peas, rinsed
¼ teaspoon freshly ground
   black pepper

1) Cut the unpeeled eggplant into rough ¾-inch cubes, place in a colander, and toss with 1 teaspoon of salt. Set aside for 20 minutes. Rinse under cold water and pat dry on several layers of paper towels.

2) Heat the olive oil in one large or two medium-sized skillets. Add the onion and cook over medium heat until it begins to soften and brown, about 5 minutes. Add the pepper and garlic and cook, stirring, for 2 minutes. Add the cumin, cinnamon, ginger, coriander, and cayenne and cook, stirring, for 1 minute. Stir in the eggplant, tomatoes, and 1 cup of water. Bring to a boil over high heat, reduce the heat to low, and cook covered, stirring occasionally, for 15 minutes.

3) Add the chick-peas and cook for another 10 to 15 minutes until the eggplant is very tender and the flavors are blended. Season with pepper and taste for salt, adding it if necessary. (Can be made 2 days ahead and refrigerated. Reheat gently before serving, adding more liquid if necessary. The dish should be slightly soupy.)

GINGERED AND CURRIED RED LENTILS

4 main-course servings

In their dried state, red lentils are probably the most beautiful of all legumes. With their saffron orangey red color and tiny, jewel-like shape they look more like ornaments than food! When cooked, red lentils change to a more subdued pale golden color and dissolve into an almost completely smooth purée, and they have a subtle, almost sweet taste all their own. Spoon these exotically spiced lentils over steamed basmati or jasmine rice, and accompany with a salad of cucumbers and tomatoes.

2 tablespoons vegetable oil
1 cup chopped onion
2 cloves garlic, chopped
1 tablespoon minced fresh
　　ginger
1 tablespoon curry powder
1 teaspoon ground cumin
1 pound red lentils, rinsed and
　　picked over

4 to 5 cups vegetable broth or
　　broth and water
¼ cup chopped cilantro or
　　parsley
½ teaspoon salt, or to taste
¼ teaspoon freshly ground
　　pepper

1) In a large, heavy saucepan, heat the vegetable oil and sauté the onion over medium-high heat, stirring frequently, until softened and browned, about 8 minutes. Add the garlic, ginger, curry powder, and cumin, and cook, stirring, for 1 minute.

2) Add the lentils and 4 cups of the broth. Bring to a boil over high heat, reduce heat to low, and cook covered until soft, 20 to 30 minutes. Add the additional broth or water if the mixture seems in danger of sticking or scorching. The lentils will almost dissolve into a smooth purée and should be slightly soupy.

3) Stir in the cilantro and season with salt and pepper. (Can be made 2 days ahead and refrigerated. Reheat gently before serving, adding a bit more liquid if necessary.)

HAVANA "MOORS AND CHRISTIANS"

6 servings

One of the staples of the Cuban diet, moros y cristianos *is a wonderfully poetic, historic name for the color combination of black beans and white rice. The beans are richly spiced (but meatless), and the dish makes great party fare, either on its own with a big salad of bright tropical vegetables and fruits, or as a side dish with roast pork or chicken.*

1 pound dried black beans, rinsed and picked over (see Note)
2 teaspoons salt
2 tablespoons olive oil
2 cups coarsely chopped onion
1 large green bell pepper, seeded and coarsely chopped
3 cloves garlic, finely chopped
2 teaspoons ground cumin
½ teaspoon cayenne
2 bay leaves
1 teaspoon sugar
1 tablespoon vinegar (any kind)
Freshly ground black pepper
2 cups raw long-grain rice
1 cup thinly sliced scallions, including green tops

1) If you like, soak the beans in water to cover for 4 hours or overnight. Drain into a colander. In a large soup pot, bring 8 cups of water to a boil. Add the soaked or unsoaked beans and 1 teaspoon of the salt, and simmer until the beans are just tender, 1 to 1½ hours. Drain, reserving the cooking liquid, and return the beans to the pot.

2) Meanwhile, in a large skillet, heat the olive oil. Add the onion and green pepper and cook until somewhat softened, about 5 minutes. Add the garlic, cumin, and cayenne and cook, stirring, for 1 minute.

3) Scrape the onion/green pepper mixture into the precooked beans. Add 3 cups of the reserved cooking liquid, along with the bay leaves and sugar. Simmer uncovered over low heat for about 30 minutes, until the beans are very tender. The beans should be quite thick but still soupy enough to ladle over the rice. Adjust the liquid as necessary. Discard the bay leaves and season with the vinegar and black pepper. (The beans can be made 2 days ahead and refrigerated. Reheat before serving with the rice, adding a bit more liquid if needed.)

4) For the rice, bring 4 cups of water to a boil in a large, heavy saucepan. Add the remaining 1 teaspoon of salt and the rice. Stir, reduce the heat to low, and cook covered until the rice is tender, about 20 minutes.

5) To serve, mound the rice on a large platter, make a well in the center, and spoon the beans into it, allowing some to spill out over the rice. Sprinkle scallions over the top.

NOTE: Canned bean option: Omit the cooking in Step 1. In Step 3, use 6 cups cooked black beans and about 3½ to 4 cups of water or broth. Simmer the black bean mixture a few mintues longer to develop flavors and thicken the sauce.

RED BEAN, SUN-DRIED TOMATO, AND MUSHROOM SAUCE ON POLENTA

4 servings

This sauce, which is kind of a quick, updated, meatless version of cacciatore (minus the chicken and plus the beans), is spooned over baked cheese polenta, that soothing, currently chic Italian cornmeal mush. This dish seems particularly appropriate served on a cool autumn evening accompanied by a salad of chicory or a mix of seasonal greens.

RED BEAN, SUN-DRIED TOMATO, AND MUSHROOM SAUCE

3 tablespoons olive oil

½ pound mushrooms, thinly sliced (see Note)

2 cloves garlic, chopped

1 (28-ounce) can crushed tomatoes in purée

¾ cup chopped or thinly sliced drained oil-packed sun-dried tomatoes

¼ cup dry white wine

2 cups drained cooked red, pink, or kidney beans, rinsed

1 teaspoon dried basil

½ teaspoon sugar

¼ teaspoon freshly ground pepper

BAKED CHEESE POLENTA

1¼ cups yellow cornmeal

½ teaspoon salt, or more to taste

⅛ teaspoon freshly ground pepper

5 tablespoons grated Parmesan cheese

1) To make the sauce, heat the olive oil in a large skillet. Add the mushrooms and cook over medium heat, stirring frequently, until lightly browned and softened, about 6 minutes. Add the garlic and cook, stirring, for 1 minute.

2) Stir in the crushed tomatoes and purée, sun-dried tomatoes, wine, beans, basil, sugar, and pepper. Bring to a boil over high heat, reduce to medium-low, and simmer uncovered for 15 minutes. Use the back of a spoon to mash about a quarter of the beans against the side of the pan to thicken the sauce. Continue to simmer for another 5 minutes or until the sauce is somewhat reduced and thickened. (Can be made 2 days ahead and refrigerated. Reheat gently before serving, adding a bit more liquid if necessary.)

3) To make the polenta, bring 2 cups of water to a boil in a large, heavy saucepan. In a medium bowl, whisk the cornmeal into 1 cup of cold water. Gradually whisk the cornmeal paste into the boiling water. Return to a boil, reduce the heat to low, and cook uncovered, whisking often, until the polenta is very thick, about 5 minutes. Whisk in the salt, pepper, and ¼ cup of the cheese.

4) Scrape the polenta into a well-seasoned 8- or 9-inch cast iron skillet or lightly greased baking dish and sprinkle with the remaining 1 tablespoon of cheese. (Can be made 8 hours ahead and refrigerated. Return to room temperature before baking.)

5) Preheat the oven to 375 degrees. Bake the polenta uncovered until it begins to pull away from the sides of the pan and the top is pale golden, about 25 minues.

6) To serve, cut the polenta in wedges and ladle the sauce over.

NOTE: Use any type of fresh mushrooms. Wild mushrooms, such as shiitake, are more flavorful, but ordinary cultivated mushrooms are fine, too.

LEMONY LENTIL STEW WITH SPINACH AND POTATOES

4 servings

Based on a Lebanese *lentil recipe, this savory meatless stew is enlivened with the sunny flavors of lemon and fresh mint. Serve it with plenty of crusty peasant bread for swabbing up every last trace of garlicky juice.*

2 cups brown or green lentils, rinsed and picked over
4 cups vegetable broth
3 tablespoons olive oil
1 cup sliced onions
3 large cloves garlic, chopped
¼ teaspoon cayenne
1 (10-ounce) package frozen chopped spinach or 1 pound fresh spinach

1½ pounds red-skinned potatoes, unpeeled, sliced ¼ inch thick (2 to 3 large potatoes)
1 teaspoon grated lemon zest
⅓ cup lemon juice
½ cup chopped fresh mint
Salt
Freshly ground black pepper

1) In a large saucepan, combine the lentils, broth, and 1 cup of water. Bring to a boil, reduce the heat to low, and simmer covered until the lentils are almost tender, about 20 minutes. (If using green lentils, cook 10 minutes longer.)

2) In another large saucepan or deep, covered skillet, heat the olive oil over medium heat. Add the onions and cook, stirring frequently, until they begin to soften, about 4 minutes. Add the garlic and cayenne and cook, stirring, for 1 minute. Add the lentils and their liquid along with the spinach and potatoes. Cook covered over medium-low heat, giving an occasional gentle stir to break up the frozen spinach, until the potatoes and lentils are tender, about 20 minutes. The consistency should be stewlike. If too much liquid has been absorbed, add a bit more liquid.

3) Stir in the lemon zest, lemon juice, and mint and season the stew with salt and pepper to taste. Serve in shallow soup bowls.

BLACK BEAN AND SWEET POTATO STEW

2 to 3 servings   **S**erve this simply deli-
*cious black and orange stew with a salad of crisp raw
vegetables such as jicama, red pepper, and romaine, tossed
with a light vinaigrette. Pass a basket of warm corn tortillas
or corn muffins.*

3 tablespoons olive oil
1 cup coarsely chopped onion
1 green bell pepper, seeded and
   coarsely chopped
2 cloves garlic, finely chopped
1 tablespoon chili powder
1½ cups diced peeled sweet
   potato (about 6 ounces)

1 (14- to 16-ounce) can Mexican-
   style stewed tomatoes
2 cups drained cooked black
   beans, rinsed
3 tablespoons chopped cilantro
½ teaspoon Tabasco
Salt
Freshly ground black pepper

1) In a large saucepan or deep, covered skillet, heat the olive oil.
Add the onion, green pepper, and garlic and cook over medium
heat until the vegetables begin to soften, about 4 minutes. Stir in the
chili powder and cook for 1 minute. Add 1 cup of water and the
sweet potato. Cover and cook until the potato can just be pierced
with a sharp knife, about 10 minutes.

2) Add the stewed tomatoes and beans, breaking the tomatoes up
into smaller chunks with the side of a spoon. Simmer the stew
uncovered over medium-low heat until the potato is very tender,
about 8 minutes. To thicken the sauce slightly, mash about a quarter
of the beans against the side of the pan.

3) Stir in the cilantro and season with Tabasco and salt and pepper
to taste.

JAMAICAN RICE 'N' PEAS WITH COCONUT MILK

6 main-course servings

This is the Caribbean *definition of comfort food — soothing, filling, but with a subtly spicy kick. In Jamaica, where it's always cooked with dark red kidney beans, they call this "rice 'n' peas," whereas on other islands the same dish, made with one of a number of other beans, is known as "peas 'n' rice." I had two talented Jamaican-born consultants giving me the benefit of their advice on this recipe: Neville Carnegie, chef, friend, and fellow soup kitchen volunteer, and musician/composer Gavin Chuck, who added the final grace notes.*

8 ounces dried red kidney beans (see Note)
1 teaspoon salt, plus additional to taste
⅔ cup coconut milk (see Note)
3 cloves garlic, finely chopped
3 tablespoons chopped fresh thyme or 1 tablespoon dried

½ a Scotch bonnet pepper or 2 jalapeño peppers, fresh or pickled, minced
¼ teaspoon ground allspice
2 cups raw long-grain rice
1 cup sliced scallions, including green tops
3 tablespoons butter
Freshly ground black pepper

1) If you like, soak the beans in water to cover for 4 hours or overnight. Drain into a colander. In a large soup pot, bring 7 cups of water to a boil. Add the soaked or unsoaked beans and 1 teaspoon salt. Cover, reduce the heat to very low, and simmer until the beans are about three quarters cooked, 1 to 1½ hours.

2) Add the coconut milk, garlic, thyme, Scotch bonnet or jalapeño pepper, and allspice and simmer for 5 minutes. Add the rice, scallions, and butter and cook covered over low heat until the liquid is absorbed and the rice is tender, about 25 minutes. Toward the end of the cooking time, add additional liquid if the rice is not yet tender and the dish seems dry.

3) Season with black pepper, and salt if necessary.

NOTE: Canned bean option: To make with canned beans, omit
Step 1. Bring 4 cups water to a boil, proceed with Step 2, and
then add 3 cups drained cooked kidney beans along with the rice.
Mash some of the beans against the side of the pot to color
the finished dish. Canned unsweetened coconut milk can now be
found in many supermarkets and is in most Asian markets.

SPICY MUNG BEAN DAL

4 servings

Called *"moong dal"* in India, these are mung beans, dried and split. One of the staple dishes in India, the beans are especially delicious cooked this way with fragrant spices and served over or alongside jasmine rice. Instructions vary on presoaking mung dal. I prefer not to soak them because the end result has a bit more texture.

1 tablespoon olive oil
1 cup chopped onion
2 cloves garlic, finely chopped
1 jalapeño or serrano pepper, minced
½ teaspoon ground coriander seed
¼ teaspoon turmeric
1 medium-large tomato, seeded and chopped (about 1 cup)

1 cup mung bean dal, rinsed and picked over
3 cups vegetable broth
3 tablespoons grated coconut, preferably unsweetened
1½ teaspoons garam masala (see Note)
⅓ cup chopped cilantro
3 cups cooked jasmine or other white rice

1) Heat the olive oil in a large, heavy saucepan. Sauté the onion over medium heat until softened and lightly browned, about 8 minutes. Add the garlic, jalapeño, coriander, and turmeric and cook, stirring, for 1 minute.

2) Add the chopped tomato, dal, broth, and coconut. Bring to a boil, skimming off any foam that rises to the surface. Simmer uncovered, stirring occasionally, until the beans are tender and the mixture is quite thick, about 30 minutes. (Can be made 3 days ahead and refrigerated. Reheat gently, adding a bit of water if necessary.)

3) Add the garam masala and simmer 5 minutes. Stir in the cilantro just before serving.

4) Serve over hot cooked rice.

NOTE: Garam masala is a mixture of fragrant ground spices and can be purchased in jars in the spice section of some supermarkets or in specialty stores.

SPICED COUSCOUS WITH CHICK-PEAS, ALMONDS, AND DATES

4 servings

This *exotically spiced vegetarian main course takes just a few minutes to put together and tastes fabulous. Try it teamed with a salad of sliced tomatoes, sweet onions, and cucumber topped with a simple dressing of plain yogurt with some chopped fresh mint stirred in.*

3 tablespoons olive oil
1 cup sliced almonds
3 cloves garlic, finely chopped
1 teaspoon paprika
1 teaspoon ground cumin
¾ teaspoon ground coriander
½ teaspoon cayenne
2½ cups vegetable broth

2 cups drained cooked chick-peas, rinsed
1 cup chopped dates
1¼ cups packaged couscous
Salt
Freshly ground black pepper
½ cup chopped scallions, including green tops

1) In a large skillet, heat the olive oil and sauté the almonds over medium heat, stirring frequently, until fragrant and lightly toasted, about 2 minutes. Add the garlic and cook, stirring, for 1 minute. Stir in the paprika, cumin, coriander, and cayenne.

2) Add the broth, chick-peas, and dates. Bring to a boil and add the couscous. Stir once to combine, cover the pan, and remove from the heat. Let stand for 5 minutes, until the couscous absorbs the liquid.

3) Fluff the couscous mixture with a fork, season with salt and pepper to taste, and sprinkle with scallions before serving.

SPRINGTIME FAVA BEAN MEDLEY

2 main-course servings

Make this delicate stew in the spring when fava beans, asparagus, tiny green beans, and new potatoes first arrive in the market. Fresh fava beans are a rare treat, and though somewhat time consuming to shell and peel, well worth the occasional effort. If you can't get them, substitute frozen lima beans. I do not recommend canned favas. They develop a strange, musty taste when canned.

1 pound unshelled (in pods) fava beans
2 tablespoons olive oil, preferably extra-virgin
2 cloves garlic, finely chopped
1 large red-skinned potato, cut in rough 1-inch dice (about 10 ounces)
1¾ cups vegetable broth
8 ounces asparagus, trimmed and cut in 1-inch lengths
4 ounces haricots verts or slender string beans, trimmed and cut in 1-inch lengths
1 tablespoon chopped fresh thyme or 1½ teaspoons dried
⅓ cup dry white wine
Salt
Freshly ground black pepper
½ cup bread crumbs, preferably from Italian or French bread
2 tablespoons Parmesan cheese

1) Shell the fava beans. (You should have about 1½ cups of shelled beans.) Cook the beans in a pot of lightly salted boiling water for 5 minutes. Drain into a colander and run under cold water. Use a sharp knife to peel the thick skin from the beans and set them aside.
2) In a large saucepan or deep skillet, heat the olive oil. Add the garlic and cook over medium heat for 1 minute. Add the potato and the vegetable broth, bring to a boil, reduce the heat, and simmer partially covered for 8 minutes. Add the asparagus, green beans, and thyme and simmer uncovered for 3 minutes.
3) Add the wine and reserved fava beans and simmer uncovered until all the vegetables are tender, 2 to 4 minutes. Season with salt and pepper to taste.
4) Toss the bread crumbs over medium heat in a small skillet until lightly toasted, 3 to 4 minutes. Off heat, toss with the cheese.
5) Serve the stew in shallow soup bowls and sprinkle with the toasted bread topping.

VEGETARIAN BRUNSWICK STEW

4 to 5 servings

This scrumptious meatless version of the classic southern stew cries out to be eaten with big, warm squares of golden corn bread, all the better to sop up the delectable gravy. Lima beans are always a traditional ingredient in Brunswick stew. If you happen to be lucky enough to get fresh lima beans, by all means use them. If not, frozen are just fine, but avoid canned limas. Like other shell beans, they don't take well to the canning process.

1 tablespoon vegetable oil
1 tablespoon butter
1½ cups chopped onion
2 cloves garlic, finely chopped
1 tablespoon all-purpose flour
2 teaspoons dried thyme
2 cups vegetable broth
1 large red-skinned potato
　　(about 8 ounces), unpeeled
　　and coarsely chopped
1 carrot, peeled and sliced

1 (10-ounce) package (2 cups)
　　frozen lima beans
1 (14- to 16-ounce) can stewed
　　tomatoes
1½ cups frozen corn kernels
1 tablespoon brown sugar
2 teaspoons Worcestershire
　　sauce
2 teaspoons cider vinegar
¼ to ½ teaspoon Tabasco

1) In a large, deep skillet or dutch oven, heat the vegetable oil and butter. Add the onion and cook over medium heat, stirring occasionally, until softened, about 5 minutes. Add the garlic and cook, stirring, 1 minute. Stir in the flour and thyme and cook, stirring constantly, for 2 minutes. Add the broth and bring to a boil, whisking until the sauce is smooth and lightly thickened.

2) Add the potato, carrot, and lima beans. Cover, reduce the heat to medium-low, and cook for 10 minutes. Add the tomatoes and corn and simmer uncovered until all the vegetables are tender, about 15 minutes. Add a bit more liquid if the stew seems too thick. It should be of a spoonable, stewlike consistency, not too soupy.

3) Stir in the brown sugar, Worcestershire, vinegar, and Tabasco. (Can be made 1 day ahead and refrigerated. Reheat gently before serving, adding a bit more liquid if necessary.)

4) Serve the stew in shallow soup bowls or on deep rimmed plates.

FIESTA TORTILLA AND BLACK BEAN CASSEROLE

4 servings

This festive casserole can be put together very quickly for a family supper but also makes great party fare when doubled or tripled and made in one large baking dish. A salad of sliced oranges and red onions, a basket of warm tortillas, and sorbet or flan for dessert would complete the meal nicely.

3 cups drained cooked black beans, rinsed
¾ cup chopped red onion
2 teaspoons chili powder
1 teaspoon ground cumin
½ cup vegetable broth or water
1 medium-large tomato, seeded and chopped (about 1 cup)
1 (4-ounce) can chopped green chiles, drained
½ teaspoon Tabasco (optional)
Vegetable oil for shallow-frying

12 (6-inch) corn tortillas
1½ cups grated sharp Cheddar cheese
1½ cups grated Monterey Jack cheese
½ cup sour cream
2 cups shredded romaine or iceberg lettuce
Good-quality chunky bottled salsa or Pico de Gallo Salsa (page 80)

1) In a food processor, combine the beans, onion, chili powder, and cumin. Pulse to mix. With the machine running, pour the broth through the feed tube and process to a coarse purée. Transfer to a bowl and stir in the tomato and green chiles. Taste for seasoning. If the green chiles were not especially hot, add the Tabasco sauce to make the purée somewhat spicy.

2) Heat about ½ inch of vegetable oil in a large frying pan over medium heat. When the oil is hot but not smoking, use tongs to immerse the tortillas in the oil, one or two at a time, until softened but not colored or crisp, about 10 to 15 seconds. Drain on paper towels.

3) Toss the grated cheeses together in a bowl. Line a shallow 2-quart baking dish with 4 overlapping tortillas. Spread with half the black bean purée and sprinkle with about ¾ cup of cheese. Top with another layer of 4 tortillas, spread with the remaining beans, and sprinkle with another ¾ cup of cheese. Top with a last layer of the remaining tortillas.

4) Whisk the sour cream into the remaining 1½ cups grated cheese. Spread the cheese-cream mixture evenly over the top layer of tortillas. (Can be made several hours ahead. Cover and refrigerate. Return to room temperature before baking.)

5) Preheat the oven to 350 degrees. Bake the casserole uncovered in the preheated oven until heated through and the topping is crusty and pale golden, 35 to 45 minutes.

6) Cut in squares and serve topped with the lettuce and salsa.

WHITE BEAN AND GREENS GRATIN

4 servings

Greens and beans play *off one another beautifully, with the soft, neutrally flavored beans acting as the perfect foil for the pleasing, slightly sour pungency of the greens. Tie the dish together with a bit of olive oil, more than a bit of garlic, and seal the top with a crust of peppery crumbs for a fabulous meatless dinner.*

PEPPERY CRUMB TOPPING
1 cup fresh bread crumbs
1 tablespoon olive oil, preferably extra-virgin
½ teaspoon black pepper, preferably coarsely ground

BEAN AND GREENS GRATIN
2 tablespoons olive oil, preferably extra-virgin
2 cloves garlic, finely chopped
1½ cups vegetable broth

2 cups drained cooked white beans such as cannellini, rinsed
1 (10-ounce) package frozen greens (turnip or mustard), thawed and drained
1 large tomato, seeded and chopped (about 1½ cups)
1 tablespoon chopped fresh thyme or 1 teaspoon dried
½ teaspoon dried leaf sage, crumbled
Salt

1) In a small bowl, toss the crumbs with the olive oil and pepper.
2) For the gratin, heat the olive oil over medium heat in a large skillet. Add the garlic and cook, stirring, 1 minute. Add the broth and beans and bring to a simmer. Mash about a quarter of the beans against the side of the pan to thicken the mixture.
3) Add the greens, tomato, thyme, and sage. Cook uncovered over medium heat until slightly reduced and thickened, 10 to 15 minutes. The mixture should be quite soupy, as it will absorb liquid as it bakes. Season with salt. (Can be made 1 day ahead and refrigerated.)
4) Preheat the oven to 375 degrees. Transfer the bean mixture to a 2-quart oval or square baking dish. Sprinkle evenly with the crumbs.
5) Bake uncovered in the preheated oven until the crumbs are crusty and lightly browned and the gratin is hot throughout, 25 to 35 minutes. If the crumbs are not quite brown enough, run the gratin under the broiler, watching carefully that they don't burn.

INDEX

Almonds, spiced couscous with chick-peas, dates and, 127
Angel's hell-fire Texas black bean caviar, 22
appetizers, dips, and snacks, 11–24
arugula, Italian sausage and white beans on, 78
Asian noodles, pork in black bean sauce on, 99

Bacon and bean sauce, penne with savory, 77
baked beans, New England "from scratch," 96–97
beef and bean tortilla pizzas with tomato-orange salsa, 68–69
black bean(s):
  Brazilian feijoada with accompaniments, streamlined, 88–89
  cakes with ragin' Cajun salsa, 16–17
  caviar, Angel's hell-fire Texas, 22
  and Cheddar nachos, 24
  dip, zesty, 15, 19
  Havana "Moors and Christians," 118–19
  orange and raisin tostadas, spiced, 66–67
  sauce, pork in, on Asian noodles, 99
  shrimp and mango salad, 58–59
  soup with chopped vegetable garnishes, 27
  sweet corn and red pepper salsa, 20
  and sweet potato stew, 123
  and tortilla casserole, fiesta, 130–31

and turkey chili verde, 86
black-eyed pea(s):
  Low Country Hoppin' John, 79
  salad with sun-dried tomato vinaigrette, 51
  and sweet onion relish, State Fair, 21
Brazilian feijoada with accompaniments, streamlined, 88–89
broccoli rabe, orecchiette with white beans and, 109
brown rice and red bean salad with hot pepper dressing, 53
Brunswick stew, vegetarian, 129
Burgundy Street red beans 'n' rice, 94–95
burritos, "never-fried" bean, with lime-grilled chicken, 64–65

Cabbage, shellfish and white bean stew with, 106
Cajun salsa, black bean cakes with ragin', 16–17
cannellini:
  grilled pizzas with tomatoes, olives and, 70–71
  "pesto" with baguette toasts, 13
  and tuna salad, Tuscan, 60
carrot, white bean and pear soup, creamy, 36
casserole, fiesta tortilla and black bean, 130–31
cassoulet with herbed pepper crumb crust, 91–93
Cheddar and black bean nachos, 24
chicken:
  chili blanco, 87
  lime-grilled, "never-fried" bean burritos with, 64–65
  and vegetable couscous, Moroccan, 102–3

orange (cont.):
  -tomato salsa, beef and bean
    tortilla pizzas with, 68–69
orecchiette with broccoli rabe
  and white beans, 109

Parmesan, potato purée, herbed
  green lentils on, 114–15
pasta e fagioli, 38–39
pea(s):
  'n' rice with coconut milk,
    Jamaican, 124–25
  potato and leek soup, sweet,
    44
  spiced Indian rice with, 112–13
pear, carrot and white bean soup,
  creamy, 36
penne with savory bean and
  bacon sauce, 77
pepper(s):
  herbed crumb crust, cassoulet
    with, 91–93
  hot, dressing, red bean and
    brown rice salad with, 53
  hot, paste, for Moroccan chicken
    and vegetable couscous, 103
  red, hummus, 14
  red, sweet corn and black bean
    salsa, 20
"pesto" cannellini with baguette
  toasts, 13
pico de gallo, classic Texas pot
  beans with, 80–81
pink adobe bean dip, spicy, 18
pink beans, simplified risotto with
  roasted garlic, tomatoes and,
  110–11
pinto bean(s):
  and beef tortilla pizzas with
    tomato-orange salsa, 68–69
  classic Texas pot beans with
    pico de gallo, 80–81

and jalapeño quesadillas, 23
and pork chili with chipotles,
  smoky, 82–83
spicy pink adobe bean dip, 18
and turkey enchiladas, mission,
  100–101
pita pockets, falafel in, with
  Middle Eastern salad, 72–73
pizzas:
  beef and bean tortilla, with
    tomato-orange salsa, 68–69
  with cannellini, tomatoes, and
    olives, grilled, 70–71
polenta, red bean, sun-dried
  tomato and mushroom sauce
  on, 120–21
pork:
  in black bean sauce on Asian
    noodles, 99
  and pinto bean chili with chipo-
    tles, smoky, 82–83
potato(es):
  lemony lentil stew with spinach
    and, 122
  Parmesan purée, herbed green
    lentils on, 114–15
  sweet pea and leek soup, 44

Ragout, cumin-scented eggplant,
  chick-pea and tomato, 116
raisin, orange and black bean
  tostadas, spiced, 66–67
red bean(s):
  and beef tortilla pizzas with
    tomato-orange salsa,
    68–69
  and brown rice salad with hot
    pepper dressing, 53
  'n' rice, Burgundy Street,
    94–95
  sun-dried tomato, and mushroom
    sauce on polenta, 120–21